The UNDERGROUND CHURCH of JERUSALEM

The UNDERGROUND CHURCH of JERUSALEM

by
ZOLA LEVITT

THOMAS NELSON INC. PUBLISHERS
Nashville • New York

Copyright © 1978 by Thomas Nelson Inc., Publishers

All rights reserved under International and Pan-American Conventions. Published in Nashville, Tennessee, by Thomas Nelson Inc. and simultaneously in Don Mills, Ontario, by Thomas Nelson & Sons (Canada) Limited.

Printed in the United States of America

Library of Congress Cataloging in Publication Data

Levitt, Zola.
   The underground church of Jerusalem.

   1. Israel—Description and travel. 2. Levitt, Zola. 3. Converts from Judaism—Biography. 4. Missions to Jews—Israel. I. Title.
DS107.4.L45   248'.246'0924 [B]   77-14970
ISBN 0-8407-5629-1

Contents

1. Brother Against Brother   9
2. I Knew Jesus Before He Was a Gentile   23
3. "The Official Resident Jew"   35
4. They Wrote the Book   47
5. Now You See It . . . The Visible Church   65
6. Now You Don't . . . The Underground Church   87
7. Some Like It Cold . . . The Quasi-Church   105
8. "Never Again!"   121
9. "Why Do the Christians Hate Us?"   137
10. "Message to America"   155

Chaverim, Shalom

Words and Music by
Zola Levitt

Slow, ad.lib. (♩ = 80)

1. Tell my brothers in Jerusalem,
2. God will bring me to Jerusalem,

Tell them I'll be coming home. When the Lord is in Je-
God will send His Shar Shalom. God will sanctify Je-

rusalem, Then, my brothers I'll be home.
rusalem. Then, my brothers I'll be home. Cha-

verim, shalom, Chaverim, Hag sameach v'shalom. When

the King comes, I'll be home! 'Til then, chaverim, shalom.

Dedicated to Dr. Gene Wheeler in gratitude
"And I will bless them that bless thee . . ."

1.
Brother Against Brother

Nineteen centuries ago, during the times of the twelve apostles, there was an underground church in Jerusalem.

It is still there.

Early Christians were abhorred in their own communities. Such anti-Christian zealots as Saul of Tarsus persecuted those steadfast believers without mercy and with the applause of the majority in the Holy Land. But they stood their ground, testified of the Messiah, and patiently built the church that was to overcome the world.

We know those first Christians were Jews—as were their principal opponents. There was a brother-against-brother struggle over the Messiah, who Himself had sadly observed, "I came not to send peace but a sword" (Matt. 10:34). He would have had it otherwise, that gentle Carpenter of Galilee, but He knew the hearts of men.

You see, I am in love with Israel. My heart is there in the homeland of my Lord. My people brought the Messiah and fought the Messiah. My people sanctified the Gentiles of the world. My people have

The Underground Church of Jerusalem

been tortured and persecuted through the ages by those who thought they were following the King of the Jews, but my people have endured.

The Feast of Tabernacles had just begun when my friend Mal Couch and I arrived in Israel for our visit with the underground church. It tells in John 7 of Jesus' trip to Jerusalem for Tabernacles. He had to go ". . . not openly, but as it were in secret." Jesus was not well liked in Jerusalem. There was virtually a price on His head.

I am not well liked in Jerusalem either, but the trip was not nearly as risky for me as it was for our King. They killed the King; I just get dirty looks.

Mal, a Gentile, can be forgiven for his Christianity. I am called a *meshumed*, a traitor.

Now I did not go to Israel to keep the Feast of Tabernacles; since I am a member of the New Covenant, I don't keep the Old Covenant feasts any longer. Jesus has fulfilled the feasts for me, as He has for all Christians. Besides, we will have a thousand years to celebrate the feast of Tabernacles in the kingdom to come: "And it shall come to pass, that everyone that is left of all the nations which came against Jerusalem shall even go up from year to year to worship the King, the Lord of hosts, and to keep the feast of tabernacles" (Zech. 14:16). God will commemorate the founding of His true tabernacle in Jerusalem with this joyful feast until the establishment of the New Jerusalem in eternity.

I went to Jerusalem for deeper, more personal reasons. I went there because I love Jerusalem and because I love my people, the Jews. I went there to find the Christians, Jewish and otherwise, and to give them my love. I went there to teach and to learn. And I went there to simply breathe the air of Jerusalem. The Jewish *Talmud* says that a man grows in wisdom when he breathes the air of Jerusalem and I believe that.

Finally, I went there because God called me to go there. Scripture relates that if a man forgets Jerusalem his right hand will "lose its cunning." If my right hand lost its cunning, I could never write again. When God calls me to Jerusalem I go! *"Hineni,"* I tell Him in the word of my father Abraham—"Here I am."

The Underground Church

My traveling companion Mal Couch, president of the Evangelical Communications Research Foundation, is a renowned Christian filmmaker and expert on Israel and the Jews. Mal's seminar—"A Walk Through the Bible"—effectively develops the Abrahamic Covenant by which God chose the Jews and ultimately sent the Messiah. Our journey's primary purpose was to offer Mal's unique Bible study along with my supplementations to the people of Jerusalem. The Jerusalem YMCA provided a place for many Jews to hear and consider a revolutionary view of God's Word.

The Israelis, we figured, would have the opportunity to digest Mal's precision with and Christian orientation toward the Scriptures along with my own Jewish love of the Messiah. Conceivably, an endorsement by me, a bearded Levite, would give Mal's beautiful renderings of the Word an added dimension. We hoped we might just possibly bring some Jew and His Savior together.

We ended up going to "church" first when we arrived in Jerusalem. We arrived on the first day of the Feast of Tabernacles, the fifteenth day of the seventh month (Friday, Oct. 8, on the 1976 gentile calendar), bushed from our international odyssey and would not have felt like working anyway. Going to church instead was fitting. As God requested, "On the first day shall be an holy convocation: ye shall do no servile work therein" (Lev. 23:35).

"Church" was held on Saturday morning (still the first day of Tabernacles because the Jewish day begins at sundown). Saturday is the Sabbath in Israel, while Sunday is a normal workday for the Jews. (The Moslems observe their Sabbath on Friday, the foreign Christians on Sunday, and I suppose some guru will arrive some day with a Tuesday or Wednesday Sabbath.)

And so Mal and I encountered our first brethren of the visible Jerusalem "church." I keep putting "church" in quotes because church is not really *church* in Israel, just as Sunday is not the Sabbath and Palestinians are not native to Palestine. Israel bears some preliminary explaining.

The term "church" really does not apply to the true church in Israel. The true *witnessing* church is largely underground since conspicuous missionary work by residents is forbidden in the Holy Land. So when an Israeli speaks of a church in Israel, he probably refers to a Protestant denominational, Catholic, or Eastern Orthodox church building into which no Jew has stepped for centuries. Those who support these institutions are not committed to evangelism; this is why they are able to keep good relations with a touchy government.

Those who desire to take the gospel to the Jews and thus are truly part of the body of Christ attend houses of worship that do not use the term "church." On that first day of Tabernacles, we went to "The Baptist House" and "The Messianic Assembly." Later in the week, we found other such meeting places of the born-again believers all bearing similar names.

So, if you're looking for *the* church in Israel, don't look for one with "church" in the name.

Though I had been to Israel previously, I had not mixed with the true church, since I had not known where to look for it. Having found it, I am as astonished by it as you will be. I am amazed by the courage of those in the witnessing church, who might suffer everything from ridicule to virtual deportation for trying to take Jesus back home. And I am thankful for the unfamiliar but oddly affecting worship services we attended all through our tour.

We attended five different Christian worship services and Bible studies in our ten days, as well as witnessing the ongoing celebration in the streets of the Feast of Tabernacles. We also went to the Wailing Wall for *Simchat Torah,* that unbelievable annual wild party wherein the Jews celebrate the fact that *they* were the nation chosen to receive God's Holy Word. We saw orthodox men in their full robes and crowns dancing in circles holding the holy *Torah* scrolls high over their heads and simply screaming with joy!

But the most joyful, most fulfilling moments we cherished were with the underground church—those true soldiers of Christ whose missionary work among the chosen people compels them to remain virtually out of sight. We were told the story of how a missionary was ferreted out in the community; a sign was placed on the apartment building of the detested one that read, BEWARE OF MISSIONARY! HIDE YOUR CHILDREN! The name and apartment number of the culprit were written on the sign. We heard of how a courageous gentile Christian woman who had gone through the agonizing ritual of converting to the Jewish faith—a massive course of study and qualification—was vilified by picketers carrying signs in front of her apartment building. This woman had become a Jewess in order to better testify of Christ, as well as to become a full-fledged citizen of Israel. She had even taken an Israeli name. But she hosted Bible studies that dealt with the New Testament in her apartment and the underground church attended. The local police protected her from the picketers on that difficult occasion. A citizen is a citizen.

Mal and I worshiped and learned and taught entirely in Jewish company, and the Messiah must have rejoiced. He will say, at the start of our kingdom, "Inasmuch as ye have done it unto one of the least of these my brethren, ye have done it unto me" (Matt. 25:40). We did not regard the underground church, which carries so heavy a cross in Jerusalem, as the *least* of Jesus' brothers, I assure you. We gladly shared with them and came out of it a lot wiser.

The Messianic Assembly held its service in Hebrew and Mal and I found it hard to follow. But after all, the very first Christian teachings heard on this earth were in Hebrew, so we couldn't complain. A huge sign across the podium bore the message, "Blessed is He who comes in the name of the Lord." Jesus said that Israel "shall not see me henceforth" until they uttered that word of praise (Matt. 23:39). This little assembly was taking no chances. When the King returns He will see that the Messianic Assembly has been ready and waiting.

At the Baptist House across town we heard a magnificent sermon in English based on Psalm 118. How good it was to be assured, "The voice of rejoicing and salvation is in the tabernacles of the righteous . . ." (v. 15). The pastor gestured to the street right outside our little building where the Jews were passing on their way to celebrate the Feast of Tabernacles even as we were studying that celebration as a glorious symbol of things to come. Someday we will enter into the Eastern Gate with the Lord and we will occupy God's true tabernacle on the earth. All this will take place not even five miles from where we were sitting that day in worship! How good it was to hear of "the gate of the Lord into which the righteous shall enter" (v. 20). How stunning it was to realize that we sat that very morning in "the tabernacle of the righteous" however humble it was.

We were truly gratified to see both the underground and the visible dimensions of the church in Israel.

The Jewish Christians were good enough, and brave enough, to attend our teaching sessions at the YMCA. Every one of them had things to fear in Jerusalem, but not all came to our meetings incognito. One young boy wore monastic robes of his own design. Having grown up among the berobed and black-suited orthodox Jews, he felt that his faith in Christ warranted a costume. He went through our meeting asking everyone individually, "Did you praise the Lord today?" He did not omit asking me and I told him I had. If this peculiar saint were around us all the time, we might have a stronger church for his reminders, but I did not envy him for his difficult calling of God. Like the dedicated Ezekiel, he was universally thought to be very strange.

As we walked through the streets of Jerusalem during our free time, Mal and I were stunned by the increased level of orthodoxy to be seen everywhere. Men carried the *lulav* branch, symbolic of the rich harvest that preceded the Feast of Tabernacles and the goodness of God to replenish the land each year. One hoary-headed old devotee passed us with what must have been the most stupefying mixture of the old and the new we had ever seen—he had a green *plastic lulav* branch, presumably good for a lifetime. It made me think of our synthetic Christmas trees we use year after year.

Near the *Mea Shearim*, the City of One Hundred Gates, where the devout orthodox reside, we saw the women wearing *sheitelim*, wigs. The wives of these sanctified ones shave their heads in a sign of obedience to their husbands and, as tradition has it, to turn off would-be tempters to adultery. The men in this exclusive community were magnificently robed, each seeming to want to outdo the others in the pure sanctity and gorgeousness of his holy attire. I saw a beige-colored, silken, floor-length gown on a crowned worshiper who carried a genuine six-foot-long *lulav*. They all hustled and bustled through the streets enroute to synagogues or to the Wall. Their long curled sideburns swung about in the breeze and their bewigged wives walked a respectful few paces behind. I had the impression that the women violated the spirit, if not the letter, of the *sheitelim* tradition by wearing the most sumptuous wigs and hats and very lovely dresses. They were submissive, yes, but they were adorned like King Solomon as well.

These devout, orthodox pilgrims from many nations, gathered here by the very promise of Almighty God, are the sworn enemies of Christian evangelism in the Holy Land. And they can be very tough enemies! They wrecked a doctor's office from wall to wall because he had performed an autopsy in violation of their law. They went around town ripping down or blotting out movie advertisements that showed the actors embracing. A brick was thrown at our car by a child who felt we had driven too close to the *Mea Shearim* boundary (we were three blocks away) too near to the Sabbath (it was three hours before sundown, the beginning of the Sabbath). The witnessing church has its work cut out for it among these orthodox descendants of God's most stiff-necked but beloved people.

The orthodox tolerate the presence of cults within Israel. On the *kibbutzim* there are Moonies—those "clean-cut" panhandlers for the Korean "messiah." There are witches in Jerusalem. A guru holds forth on the Mount of Olives. But if you want to cross over the line of decency with these sanctified ones, show them a Christian. Then they see red!

The Underground Church of Jerusalem

In their schools they use the letter "T" instead of the plus sign in arithmetic, the latter being too reminiscent of the hated cross of Christ.

Evangelism, anyone?

There is perhaps no more difficult mission field in the world. When those unfortunate drunken souls found in the gutters of the New York City Bowery are dried out, they hear the gospel and eat their soup in peace. When the headhunters of New Guinea see war and disease and starvation abate, they give the missionary a hearing.

But who goes to the *Mea Shearim?*

Speaking of Abraham's descendants, God said, "I will bless them that bless thee" (Gen. 12:3). Few seek this particularly hard-fought blessing. Except for a visiting missionary here and there, whose visa may be canceled at any moment, only the underground church of Jerusalem carries the burden of the Messiah for His brothers in this hard field.

Books are available through a few Christian bookstores (operating under various pseudonyms) and these do carry out a witness. God, after all, chose to use books. Hal Lindsey's *Late, Great Planet Earth* is there in Hebrew and English for those who wish to know his concept of the future of Israel and the world. Mal and I lavishly passed out free copies to the Jews. We were gratified to see my own books on the shelves of Jerusalem bookstalls, particularly the inflammatory *Jesus, The Jew's Jew*, which must almost rate as pornography. But understandably, we saw little one-on-one telling of the gospel.

We were privileged to witness to the native Israelis and the tourists who came to our Bible study, and to the massive and frightening crowd of 600 who came out for our film night. In the providence of God we were able to witness to a robed, orthodox, eighty-year-old Jew in the *Mea Shearim* and he promised to prayerfully consider Yeshua of Nazareth. We also attended a Sabbath dinner, a tradition going back to Peter and Paul, where the Christians meet in fellowship, testimony, and song. And we breathed a lot of the wonderful air of Jerusalem.

The Road of Courage

As I walked the streets of Jerusalem I was troubled, as is any Jew who visits his true homeland. *Shouldn't I be there?* the Jew must ask himself as he returns to air-conditioned America. *Shouldn't I build the land with my brothers?*

Who can know the mind of God? He did not choose to call Paul to Israel but sent him to a foreign field instead. I have a ministry in a foreign field and, like Paul, I was born away from the homeland. It is perfectly reasonable that I write my books in the English language and conduct my work for God in America.

But rationalizing does not quiet the still, small voice of Abraham within us all. "I went to Israel," he whispers in our Jewish hearts. "I told God, '*Hineni*,' and I traveled far."

I passed the many military cemeteries of the war-torn Promised Land. I passed the place in the road where seventy-seven unarmed Jewish doctors and nurses were shot down trying to reach a field hospital during the War of Independence in 1948. I drove over the Road of Courage, the highway laid by hand by the women and children and old men of the Judean villages. When the enemy had cut the main highway from Tel Aviv to Jerusalem, these defiant ones, scornful of the steady fire of the Arab machine guns, built a road 120 kilometers long. There were few survivors, but their Road of Courage will honor and glorify the kingdom in Israel during Christ's millenial reign on earth.

These reminders of the past cause deeply troubling moments for the returning Jew. He goes back to the relative peace of America or Europe, leaving his few brothers to guarantee the borders of the Promised Land. And for the Jewish Christian, he shirks an empty mission field as well.

Should I have stayed there? Before I grow old and my right hand loses its cunning altogether, shouldn't I use it for the Promised Land? If the poor young widows of Israel can build a road, surely I can find something to do for my people.

But then, they will hate me if I go there because I will testify of my Lord. How can I not witness to them? How could I condemn them to death by keeping my mouth shut? Paul cried, "How shall they hear without a preacher?" (Rom. 10:14). He also said, "My heart's desire and prayer to God for Israel is that they might be saved" (Rom. 10:1), and, "Hath God cast away his people? God forbid!" (Rom. 11:1). He said the gospel was supposed to go "to the Jew first" (Rom. 1:16).

I asked God, "Where can I be more effective for my people?" Here in America I can write freely about Christ and witness to the Jews all I want—nobody's going to throw me out of the country for believing in Jesus. I don't have much company, but I can go to the

Brother Against Brother

Jews at will. In Israel I would be an outcast if I did my work well. Once they knew me, they wouldn't even want me to build a road.

Exhausted with the conflict, I took out a sheet of paper and began to compose a song. God speaks to me reliably through music, and the answer to my dilemma was right there when I finished:

> Tell my brothers in Jerusalem,
> Tell them I'll be coming home.
> When the Lord is in Jerusalem
> Then, my brothers, I'll be home.
>
> God will bring me to Jerusalem.
> God will send His *Sar Shalom.**
> God will sanctify Jerusalem.
> Then, my brothers, I'll be home.
>
> *Chaverim, shalom.*
> *Chaverim, hag sameach v'shalom.*
> When the King comes, I'll be home
> Til then, *chaverim, shalom.*

*Translation from the Hebrew: *Sar Shalom*, Prince of Peace. *Chaverim, shalom*, Brothers, peace. *Hag sameach*, Happy Holy Days.

2.
I Knew Jesus Before He Was a Gentile

Things were not always so tough in the Christian church of Jerusalem. The Jews weren't always so hard on Christian missionaries.

As a matter of fact, there once was a time when the whole church of Jerusalem was Jewish and all the missionaries who went out were Jews. You may not have to be Jewish to love rye bread, but there was a time you had to be Jewish to love Jesus!

I refer to the ministry of the Messiah and its immediate results. Back then, Jesus was still Jewish.

The coming of Christ, a radical Jew Himself, caught many Jews unawares. The majority of Israel just could not believe that salvation was free for the asking. But even a cursory examination of the Bible would have told them that Christianity, as well as its Deliverer, was entirely Jewish.

Jeremiah prophesied the advent of Christianity in Israel in his stirring announcement on behalf of God, ". . . I will make a new covenant with the house of Israel, and with the house of Judah" (Jer. 31:31). Paul carefully repeated these exact words in Hebrews 8:8 for the benefit of those who may have overlooked them. The New Covenant, under which God would "forgive their iniquity," and "remember their sin no more" (Jer. 31:34; Heb. 8:12) was made with the Jews, as were all covenants since Abraham. Israel was to be saved.

All of God's covenants were signed in blood; in contracting with Abraham, Moses, and David, God required an animal sacrifice to seal the promises between Himself and the Jews. Just so, Jesus' crucifixion was the blood sacrifice which ratified the extraordinary New Covenant.

Jesus announced plainly, "I am not sent but unto the lost sheep of the house of Israel" (Matt. 15:24). This was reasonable. If the covenant was to be made with Israel, He certainly would not go to the Gentiles. They were not even aware of any such covenant. Therefore Jesus instructed His disciples, "Go not into the way of the Gentiles" (Matt. 10:5), and He dealt almost exclusively with the Jews.

True, a few Gentiles approached the miracle-working Preacher of Galilee and He perceived their faith and granted them forgiveness. The Canaanite woman's daughter was healed, as was the Roman centurion's servant; the testimony of the astonished woman at the well in Samaria galvanized her whole village and many people were saved. Jesus turned away no one, but He *came* to His own.

The words "testament" and "covenant" are the same. The New Testament is simply our copy of the contract—the New Covenant. It relates to the salvation of those Jews who received the Messiah and their subsequent mission to the Gentiles of surrounding lands. It gives the terms for salvation and practical examples of how to live the faith. It especially narrates the powerful outreach of the mighty church of Jerusalem, the world's first Christian church. It supplies the interesting fact that "salvation is of the Jews" (John 4:22). The New Testament also provides prophecy to the effect that Israel will finally sanctify the world, as was God's original ideal for this unique people (Rev. 7).

Times have changed. The church of Jerusalem, once the very headquarters of Christianity, is now underground and running scared. To better understand its foundations, let's look back a moment to the days when the Jewish Christians exported salvation in Jesus Christ to the known world. We get quite a different picture of things as we see the church of Jerusalem entirely in Jewish hands. We realize with some surprise that Gentiles are in the church today because of the efforts of the Jews of Jerusalem.

All the people saved as a result of Peter's electrifying sermon at Pentecost were Jews, as were the 5,000 saved in the ensuing days when Peter and John healed the lame beggar at the temple gate (Acts 2–4). Three thousand Jews were killed on that awful day when Moses came down from Mount Sinai with the law and found the people worshiping a golden calf. But when God first poured out the Holy Spirit on Israel, 3,000 were saved. "The letter kills, but the spirit gives life" (2 Cor. 3:6).

So at least 8,000 Jewish people must have made up the membership of the church of Jerusalem. Surely those few faithful Gentiles who had appreciated the

The Underground Church of Jerusalem

ministry of the Lord were also welcome. The Lord, after all, had cited a Gentile as possessing *superior* faith in the case of the centurion: "I have not found so great faith, no, not in Israel" (Luke 7:9), He told the stunned chosen people on that occasion. That Roman policeman could have taught the Jews about true worship of God, the Messiah said in effect, and so it is certain that non-Jewish Christians were welcome in the church.

But actual witnessing to Gentiles was something else. Why take a covenant made with the house of Israel to Gentiles? They weren't even waiting for a Messiah, so why try to convert them?

We gather from the Book of Acts that the church of Jerusalem did not think in terms of bringing in Gentiles at the beginning. When Peter is summoned to the home of Cornelius in Caesarea, a whole new issue is opened up in Christianity. The tenth chapter of Acts is one of the greatest turning points in the Bible; in a remarkable and unpredictable way, God, through the words of a Jewish apostle, brought Gentiles to Jesus Christ.

The salvation of Cornelius and his friends may not come as much of a surprise to us today, but it must have really caused consternation among the Jewish church fathers back in Jerusalem. We are told that it did.

Peter taught the gospel briefly but with great effect to Cornelius and his friends. As we follow Peter through the Book of Acts his sermons grow shorter as his harvests grow larger. At Pentecost he spoke for about five minutes and 3,000 were saved. He spoke about three minutes in Acts 3 and 5,000 were saved.

Now, in Acts 10, salvation came before the apostle had even finished! "While Peter yet spake these words, the Holy Ghost fell on all them which heard the word" (Acts 10:44).

But now we get the picture of how strange it was for Gentiles to come to Christ: "And they of the circumcision which believed were astonished, as many as came with Peter, because that on the Gentiles also was poured out the gift of the Holy Ghost. For they heard them speak with tongues, and magnify God . . ." (Acts 10:45,46).

The Jewish Christians who accompanied Peter were "astonished" by what they were seeing—Gentiles receiving the Holy Spirit. Yet, as the text points out, they heard the tongues just as at Pentecost; obviously the conversions were authentic.

What about that? *Gentiles* becoming Christians?

The following verse is filled with tact, as Peter asks, "Can any man forbid water, that these should not be baptized, which have received the Holy Ghost as well as we?" (Acts 10:47).

What a question! That wasn't Peter's attitude back at Pentecost. Back then he had 3,000 new believers on his hands but he exclaimed joyfully, "Repent and be baptized!" We can imagine him shouting on that great occasion, "Let's get some water up here and baptize these new believers!"

But Cornelius and company were Gentiles!

Peter's associates honestly had no experience seeing Gentiles come to faith in Christ, speaking in tongues, and magnifying God, and so Peter asks if anyone has any objections to their proceeding normally with baptism! He even puts an argument in

The Underground Church of Jerusalem

their favor into his question—" [They] have received the Holy Ghost as well as we."

It's a funny moment in the New Testament. We could only copy the feeling today by seeing a multitude of Jewish people come to Christ all at once, and who has ever seen *that*? At any rate, the baptisms were held and the new believers discipled for several days (Acts 10:48). And somehow the news got back to the church fathers in Jerusalem.

Now we come to the punchline. The Jewish churchmen of Jerusalem, those hearty, revolutionary believers in Christ, did not particularly rejoice over this conversion of Gentiles. We can see by reading the following chapter, Acts 11, that they needed quite a bit of instruction from Peter before they could fathom that God even *wanted* Gentiles to be Christians.

How times change! The religious folk of Jerusalem today say, "Don't convert the Jews!" Back then they were saying, "Don't convert the Gentiles!" They were Jews then, and they are Jews now. The difference, of course, is that the once-mighty Christian church of Jerusalem has had to go underground and has only a quiet voice in Jesus' native land today.

Acts 11 presents a scene often played out in reverse these days. It tells us that when Peter returned to Jerusalem the Jewish Christians "contended with him, saying, Thou wentest into men uncircumcised and didst eat with them" (Acts 11:2–3).

How careful they were with Peter, to whom they were indebted for virtually their entire church membership. They certainly did not begin by criticizing so consummate a master of evangelism, a Christian apostle of stature, and the daily companion of the Lord Jesus for more than three years. No, instead they brought up a fine point of Jewish law. They wanted to scream, "How could you do it! How could you share *our* faith with Gentiles!" But instead they questioned the distinguished missionary very gently about eating in an unclean household. They might as well have said cautiously, "We hear you stopped for lunch in Caesarea."

Peter did not stop to discuss the point of law, which had become moot in view of the vision he had had from God. He imparted the vision—that scene of a picnic of unkosher foods descending from heaven on a sheet. He included his own arguments with God about eating such foods—how objectionable he found the distasteful display. But God had answered, "What God has cleansed, that call not thou common" (Acts 11:9).

Immediately following his vision Peter received the servants from Caesarea who asked him to visit their master Cornelius. The matter was clear. God was going to call out the Gentiles. They were cleansed. They could enter the New Covenant along with Israel. They were to be grafted in.

To the credit of the churchmen, ". . . they held their peace and glorified God, saying, Then hath God granted repentance unto life to the Gentiles also." That verse, Acts 11:18, is the first in the Bible that plainly states that Gentiles may be saved.

The way that scene becomes played out in reverse today is when the *gentile* churchmen find evangelism to the *Jews* somehow not in the best of taste. It would be fine if Acts 11:18 could be repeated in reverse, "Then hath God granted repentance unto life to the *Jews*" because He certainly has!

The Christian church of Jerusalem "glorified God" by recognizing the gentile claim to eternal life and immediately mounting mighty missions to all Asia and the Mediterranean. The apostles went out—Peter, Barnabas, James, John, Timothy, Titus, and the indefatigable Paul—and churches were established among the Gentiles. That Jewish work—those Jewish missions to the Gentiles—still has its effect today. Every saved non-Jewish human being can thank the faithful Jewish church of Jerusalem for those early missions, under terrible privation, that brought the gospel to the world.

But eventually an awful thing happened back in Jerusalem. The Romans invaded and razed the temple and the city. Israel was vanquished and dispersed. People stopped witnessing to the Jews somehow. They quickly forgot where their own faith had come from and they continued in churches outside the land that became increasingly gentile.

Paul, called to witness to Gentiles, could only cry, "The gospel . . . is the power of God unto salvation . . . to the Jew first . . ." (Rom. 1:16)!

Paul appealed plaintively to the church at Rome, "Brethren, my heart's desire and prayer to God for Israel is that they might be saved" (Rom. 10:1). And more forcefully, in Romans 11:1, Paul said, "I say then, Hath God cast away His people? God forbid! For I also am an Israelite, of the seed of Abraham, of the tribe of Benjamin."

Paul is having to point out, "Can you not see that *I*

am Jewish!" The witness to the Jews must have grown so lax even at that time that Paul, a missionary to the Gentiles, had to make an appeal in this heartfelt way.

Sharing Paul's Burden

And that is why I went to Jerusalem with Mal.

I also am an Israelite, of the seed of Abraham, of the tribe of Levi.* I don't think God has cast out His chosen people either.

In fact, I know He hasn't! *Am Yisroel chai!* The Jewish people lives!

I went to Israel because I am responsible to the Jews. And that is not because I am Jewish but because I am Christian. Every follower of Christ is responsible for His brothers, as He said (Matt. 25:40), and those who love God must love those He loves.

How God loves Israel! A reading of the Old Testament shows wayward children in the Holy Land indeed, but were there ever children so loved by their Father? Sins, irreverence, and idolatry all plague the history of the Jews, just as they plague the history of the Christians, but God said many times, "I will never forsake them!" (Jer. 31:37 et. al.)

When the Lord returns to establish His kingdom, "all Israel will be saved," exulted Paul (Rom. 11:26). But in the meantime, *somebody* has got to care about Jerusalem!

God has put the Jews into the care of the church in this age. The Christian church holds the key to Jewish salvation, just as the Jews once held the key to world

---

*My last name in Hebrew—*HaLevi*—means "the Levite." It probably goes back to Aaron; Levites did not tend to change their names.

salvation. If only the church would now respond as the Jews did back then; if only we could return the favor!

I was wondering just how much responsibility I, an American, have for the Jews of Israel. After all, we have plenty of Jews here that nobody cares about; I am kept pretty busy. They told my father when he tried to settle in New York City as an immigrant in 1911, "We have too many Jews *now*," and so he settled in Pittsburgh.

There are lots of Jews in this country and in the world over, but somehow my heart turns back to Israel. I went on this particular trip to examine myself in relation to my responsibility.

And secondly, I wanted to see if there really is a body of Christ in the Holy Land as there certainly once was. I know there are Christians scattered throughout Israel, but an effective body of Christ witnessing to the *Mea Shearim* is something else again. Are there Christians willing to work at it? Is the Word of the Lord going out enough to make a difference? Do the orthodox Jewish powers have the believers intimidated or do they continue the ministry in the face of all odds, even as the Lord Himself had done? Is Jesus still living in His homeland?

Ironically, though the gospel is supposed to go to the Jew first, it seems that the Jews have heard less gospel than anyone else. The gospel actually goes to them last, I think. We have many great missionary foundations studying the tongues of bushmen and islanders everywhere in the world; we have brave smugglers who take Bibles into Russia and China, and we have those tireless workers among the poor and destitute everywhere. But missions to the Jews are so few. Do you even *know* a Jewish missionary? If your Jewish friend said, "All right, I'll listen to an explanation of the gospel; send your man around," would you know where to contact your man?

Israel is your land, believer; it is your kingdom. It is the land where the Lord will establish His ruling house, His tabernacle on earth. We, His bride and His fellow rulers of the kingdom to come, will have much to do with Israel. If Israel were not in the news every day as God's prophetic plan unfolds in the Middle East, would you even know where to find it on a map?

Probably you don't have the commitment to Israel that a Jew has, and that is understandable at the moment. But I am a Jew. I am very deeply concerned. I learn from Israel; I teach about Israel; I eat, sleep, and drink Israel in every way that I can, and this is my calling. Forgive me if I press the point to what seems like an unreasonable extreme, but I am more concerned about the salvation of Israel than about the well-being of the American church. And in this I think I am lined up with God.

3.
"The Official Resident Jew"

In my work nobody really likes me. I have nothing but dissatisfied customers.

Most of my customers are Gentiles who have become Christians, and I am out to convince them to witness to the Jews. They don't really want to. It's like trying to get up a tour to a leper colony. The rest of my customers are Jews. I try to convince them that Gentiles like them, and they think I need a psychiatrist. I tell them to come to Christ and it's like offering them a case of the swine flu.

If God really wants, as He says, Jew and Gentile "one in Christ," we're doing a very bad job of it on both sides.

God pictures His ideal Christian church in Ephesians 2. In the Old Covenant, He had strictly separated Jew and Gentile. Once He contracted with Abraham to sanctify the Jewish nation there was no turning back. The Jews were to be a people set apart; they weren't even to make inquiry about gentile customs and worship practices. "I am a jealous God," God said frankly. He made a wall of partition in the temple.

His plan, as He announced it, was to sanctify the Jews first and then use them as a blessing to the rest of the world (Gen. 12:1–3). The Gentiles would become envious of Jewish blessings and would be impressed to consider the Jewish God, as things were supposed to happen.

But it did not work out that way. Israel became idolatrous and the chosen people fell out of fellowship with God. God made the New Covenant then, sending the Messiah to Israel and undertaking a new start toward Jewish sanctification of the world.

Significantly, the Messiah broke down the wall of partition that had previously separated the Jew and Gentile in God's house. Paul said, "For He is our peace, who hath made both one, and hath broken down the middle wall of partition between us" (Eph. 2:14). Those unfamiliar with the design of the temple may fail to appreciate that this wall was a reality; there was an outer court where gentile tourists gathered to appreciate the magnificent structure, but it was separated from the Jewish worship areas by a stone wall. Christ achieved the dissolution of this wall, and of all differences between what were formerly two kinds of men—Jew and Gentile. Now everyone on earth was to be sanctified equally through coming to Christ.

Paul gave God's specifications for church-building: "For through Him we both have access by one Spirit unto the Father . . . And are built upon the foundation of the apostles and prophets, Jesus Christ Himself being the chief corner stone; in whom all the building fitly framed together groweth unto an holy temple in the Lord" (Eph. 2:18,20,21).

"The Official Resident Jew"

The meaning is very clear—we're supposed to have Jews and Gentiles together in the Christian church.

But it's not happening. We aren't even close.

I go from church to church in my speaking ministry and I gather good crowds. A great many Christians come out to see the Jew who came to Christ. I teach simple biblical truths and I beg the congregations to testify to their Jewish friends. Sometimes they do, but sometimes the pastor gives me an indulgent smile which tells me it will be business as usual after I leave.

I tell the congregations, "You *must* at least say the name of the Lord to a Jew. They did it for you!" I tell them, "The Jews can be saved, very often, but nobody ever tries." I remind them, "I can't come back every Sunday; you'll have to get your own Jew!"

One church presented me with a plaque appointing me "The Official Resident Jew," and this was a good church. They did witness to the Jews around them and brought a number of them to salvation in Christ. They now have a greatly expanded congregation and a new building, as I expected. ("I will bless them that bless thee.")

What breaks my heart—what sent me to Israel for more and more evidence and information to inspire them to witness—is that I can not get through to gentile Christians most of the time. The church refuses to extend a witness to God's chosen people and so the church remains very weak.

Let's face it; God equipped the Jews when He chose them. Since He called them to be a witness to the world, He gave them the means. Look at the Jews around you—they're influential, potent people. The

The Underground Church of Jerusalem

Jews are smart and steady—they weather anything and they continue to prosper and to influence the world. They survived hundreds of oppressive powers in their 4,000 years of persecution and they know how to deal with men.

A Jew invented capitalism, a Jew invented communism. A Jew conquered polio, and Jewish doctors and medicines have revolutionized the public health of the world. (Didn't God present the first and best public health laws to the Jews in the Pentateuch?) The Jews are one-half of one percent of the population but they have won twenty percent of the Nobel prizes.*

We all know the local Jew best as a salesman, and this must be part of God's plan too. The Jew is supposed to be utilizing that marvelous business talent for "selling" the gospel. If the Jew were taking Christ to the world as he takes garments and jewelry and banking to the world, the Christian church would be mighty indeed. But since the Jew does not know Christ, he wastes that God-given talent on material goods and the majority of the world drifts along without the gospel.

Believe me, I know what would happen if the church would finally break down and enlist the Jews. The church would be a better place. Do you want to balance your church budget? Save the Jew—he knows how. Do you want to get pornography out of your community? Save the Jew—he owns the building where they sell the dirty books. Do you really want to take the gospel to all nations? Save the Jew—God hand-picked him for this task. The Jew already lives

---

*Facts in this paragraph are taken from Richard Wurmbrand's *Christ on the Jewish Road* (Glendale, Calif.: Diane Books, 1973).

in all nations and knows the languages. What we could do with another set of Peter-and-Paul style apostles these days!

I witness to individual Jews and I know it isn't easy. People call me all the time to go out to lunch with their doctor or insurance man or lawyer or boss; I am the one who supposedly knows how to crack the tough cases. Conversions sometimes do result as they will when *anybody* witnesses to the Jews, but people call me in for the open-heart surgery instead of doing it themselves.

Religion and Politics in Israel

I mention these concerns because they were an important part of the reason for my trip to Israel. I need firsthand information about things in the Holy Land, both to witness to the Jews myself and to tell others how to witness to them. Israel is close to every Jew's heart, unless he has become an utter atheist, and I want to keep abreast of developments there.

I was mainly interested in three relatively new issues in Israel these days. First, the aversion to Christian evangelism has been growing. Jews don't persecute Christians, but some recent incidents have indicated that the climate for witnessing has grown exceedingly cool. A gentile believer was involved in a court case on whether a Jew can believe in Jesus and still be a Jew; the decision went against him. That's a bad sign for evangelism in general.

Secondly, I was interested in examining the orthodox community in Israel because it has enjoyed a resurgence. Orthodox Judaism has always been the minority persuasion in the Holy Land and elsewhere throughout the world. But the militant orthodox, who have quite a voice in government and religious circles in Israel, have made great strides recently. They have become increasingly vocal with regard to political policy in Israel and their views are taken more and more seriously.

Although the orthodox are the most biblical of Jews, they are staunch enemies of evangelism. One might assume that a Bible-reading Jew would give more credence to Jesus as the Messiah in view of the weight of prophecy pointing to the First Advent of the Lord. But the orthodox Jews tend to be more expert on the commentaries than on the Scriptures. As might be expected, the commentaries seek to avoid Jesus at all costs.

And thirdly, I was interested in the political implications of religion in the Middle East in general. A phenomenon of Middle-Eastern culture that is hard to appreciate here in the States is that the governments and the religions are inextricably bound together over there, as opposed to their studied separation here. Israel's government is sensitive to Judaism, Saudi Arabia's to Islam, and so forth. In Libya, Colonel Gaddafi carries the Koran to what seems like wretched excess in leading his arcane society of robed zealots. They still demean women; they cut off the hands of thieves. Holy war against the Jews becomes sacred in those backward circles.

I have become deeply concerned about religion going political in Israel. Political religion is a sign of the Tribulation period, when the Antichrist will dictate to the world how all men must worship. The

"The Official Resident Jew"

merging of state and church that the Antichrist will achieve will facilitate his control of all human beings. (Rev. Sun Myung Moon, the "messiah" from Korea, preaches that a perfect merging of state and church will bring in the kingdom of God. We must "test the spirits"—1 John 4:1.)

Israel is not aiming at a complete merging of state and religion simply because most Israelis are not religious. If the orthodox Jews had their way, everyone would wear costumes and worship according to the law, but the fact is a great many Israelis are not interested in God. Their prime interest is in forming a strong, modern nation, which these days means a totally secular state. Israel's government is realistic and it governs all the people according to majority wishes. But the orthodox have a political party which has gained surprising strength recently and has been able to influence important legislation. Their aversion to evangelism is one of the most solid planks in their platform, and as long as they have the power they do, things will be tough on true Christians.

It is possible that if the orthodox had their way, there would not be a church of any kind allowed to remain in Israel. But Israel is a peculiar place, dotted with the holy sites of endless sects of Christianity and Islam, and the Israelis, orthodox and secular alike, must put up with the presence of the *goyim* (Gentiles) among them.

Then again, tourism is one of Israel's major industries and it would be shot to pieces without the churches and the sacred sites. Christian people go to Israel to see Christian things, not Jewish things (misunderstanding that all truly Christian things are also truly Jewish things). Jewish tourists enjoy the Sea of Galilee, locally referred to as "the lake," for a swim; Christian tourists come to gaze upon the water where the Lord once walked. The Christians would simply stop coming if the orthodox had their way, but this would never happen.

With the Moslems, things are much more serious. Any threat to the Dome of the Rock or the El Aksa Mosque, both planted firmly on the site of the ancient Jewish temples, would bring all-out war immediately. Any orthodox Jew worth his salt detests the presence of the Islam holy places on the mountain of the Lord where tradition says Abraham offered Isaac in sacrifice, but nothing, so far, can be done about the situation.

Recently, the government has been brought into religious struggles because of Jewish prayer being offered beside the Islam buildings. Some Jews have gone up on the mount to pray, particularly for *Tisha B'Av*, the sad holy day that commemorates the destruction of the two past temples.

Normally, Jewish prayer is restricted to the Western Wall, called the "Wailing Wall" by those who think Jews wail. This is a retaining wall for the mount, located below the summit where the sanctuary used to be. It was captured in the Six-Day War of 1967 and has been utilized since as the prime Jewish holy site. Jews have always been forbidden by the orthodox to go up on the mount itself since it is hopelessly desecrated by the presence of the pagan shrines. Even Gentiles are forbidden but they go up anyway, as tourists. The orthodox shrug it off—"What can you expect from them?" The Moslems, of course, go up five times a day for prayer according to their religion. They feel they have a God-given right to the summit, as well as to the rest of Jerusalem and all of Israel.

The temple mount is a one-of-a-kind trouble spot today. To say the situation is touchy is an extreme understatement. On this thirty-four acre plot of land which God has seen fit to sanctify, Jews, Christians, and Moslems come together in uneasy alliance. The place is potentially explosive every day of the year.

On a previous Israel tour, I watched the solemn ceremony of *Tisha B'Av* as it was held on the ground before the Western Wall. Ten thousand people came to pray that night, sitting on mats and crying with Jeremiah over the destruction of the temple. The Book of Lamentations was wept aloud by most of the mourners; the cries of some were truly from the heart. Suddenly, the crackling recording of the Moslem call to worship blared forth from the mount above, overwhelming the quiet weeping of the orthodox Jews below. To say that the orthodox would like to see that Dome out of there is another understatement.

But let's get back to the Jews who actually went up on the mount. What they did was considered illegal, but they purposely wanted the case tried. The police gently removed the worshipers, but not before the Jews had made their point: this was Jewish ground. The government was presented with quite a headache.

The arrested worshipers had a right to a trial and a magistrate presided over the case. She heard their arguments for the Jewish right to offer prayer on

Mount Moriah, and she ruled in their favor. Indeed, the Jews have the right to pray on the mount, regardless of the sort of shrine up there at the moment.

Jews have prayed on that mountain since Abraham and Isaac, throughout the Old Testament times, after Titus and the destruction by the Romans in A.D. 70, in spite of the placing of Hadrian's Temple of Jupiter on the mount in the second century, in the face of the Moslems with their new Dome in the seventh century, fearlessly in front of the Knights Templar in the days of the Crusades, and all through the times of the Turks, the Arabs, the British, and on and on. There haven't been *many* Jews up on the mount during the long dispersion of the chosen people, but there always have been *some*.

They see no reason to stop now.

And neither did the magistrate.

But that caused real consternation among the Moslems. There followed immediate uprisings on the West Bank and through the Arab villages. The protest was heartfelt: this, the Moslems thought, was too much.

But the small group of Jewish zealots continued to go up on the mount, now legally if not very tactfully, and matters grew worse. During my recent tour, Mal and I had to endure a long, long bus ride back from Masada to Jerusalem; the normal route goes through Hebron, now an Arab town, but the Army stopped our bus and turned us south, away from the smoldering Moslems. The soldiers could not guarantee safe passage of the tourist bus at night.

The reason for all of this is the religious-political situation, the most volatile in the Middle East. Oil and

"The Official Resident Jew"

all of its ramifications make materialistic people mad; religious violations make everybody mad.

Trouble with the Moslems is historic, but trouble with the Christians brings a new dimension to Israeli conflicts. The Moslems never try to convert anybody, or at least they certainly never try to convert the Jews. But Christians, if they are Christians worthy of the name, try to convert everybody. Moslems hear a witness more readily than Jews, but Israelis, under the circumstances, really lose patience with witnessing Christians.

You have to hand it to the government of little Israel. They have some very busy days.

I visited Israel because I needed to become more intimately acquainted with all of these conflicts. American Christians ask me questions like "How are things going with the Moslems?" and "How are things going with the Christians?" But rarely do they ask, "How are things going with our mission?" since hardly anybody ever sends a mission to Israel.

I needed to talk to the people of Israel about the government, the religious situation, and particularly the underground church. I needed to ask young men what they thought the future held, and I was able to do that.

Of course, I could not go to Israel just to study the place. I wanted to offer them something too. Mal and I planned what we would try to teach at the YMCA and how we could make the best impression for Christ. There is so much Bible to teach and most Jews have little Bible knowledge. If you had fifteen hours to talk to Jews in Jerusalem, what would *you* say? We put together the most effective program possible, using both Mal's "A Walk Through the Bible" seminar and my carefully thought-out remarks as a Jewish Christian. Finally, we put a whole evening into screening our films in search of the right ones for use in Israel.

We were mindful of the fact that Christians have never had ample time in Jerusalem. Our Lord had to accomplish the utter redirection of God's plans, from the Old Covenant to the New, in a mere three years. We were mindful too that He had to walk there a wanted man but He still went and He still taught, giving all He had.

We prayerfully planned the kind of Bible study that would provide the most vital information in the shortest possible time. We would look to the Holy Spirit to lead when it came to evangelism and to the good graces of the longsuffering people of Israel to give us a fair hearing.

4.
They Wrote the Book

Weeks before our trip I was already intimidated by the very idea of going to Israel to teach Bible.

After all, "they wrote the Book," as the expression goes. And that's the literal truth in this case.

True, the Israeli view of the Bible is lacking. Apart from a few real experts in Old Testament Scripture, the people of Israel are unfamiliar with the Bible. I wouldn't expect the man on the street to be able to give a cohesive picture of prophecy, which deeply involves Israel, or even to be able to cite the passages that give the Jews the grant to the land itself. Israeli biblical history is only vaguely understood by the ordinary citizen, but this is probably true of the ordinary citizens of other lands as well. And the New Testament is either not read at all or completely misunderstood in content and purpose.

But where does one start when teaching the people who wrote the Book?

We certainly did not want to go to Israel to offend our hosts; we wanted to be tactful but honest about what the Scriptures said. We would not shirk to identify the Messiah by name since the Bible identifies

Him plainly in both Testaments, and we would not conceal our own position for anybody's benefit. But we also wanted to have respect for the sensitivities of our pupils. For example, "Messiah" is a far better term than "Savior" in this setting. "The Palestinian Covenant" are fighting words, although this covenant gave Israel to the Jews. Even the seemingly innocuous "Old Testament" is not really appropriate in Israel—it's the "Testament"; when did it grow "old"?

Since Mal's walk through the Bible was to be the basis for our whole curriculum I began to think about what I could insert into that effective presentation of Jewish redemption. Out of the several topics I typically teach in the churches only a few would be effective with Jews—most of the topics are designed to stir up sleeping Gentiles. I certainly didn't want to belabor the Tribulation period in Israel—that would be putting the worst foot forward. Nor did I want to discuss the Rapture of the church with unsaved people. Teaching the coming restoration of the temple might have been appropriate, especially in view of the presence of the Feast of Tabernacles, but that would involve introducing the Antichrist and his covenant with Israel.

I wanted to avoid a repeated gentile-Christian blunder with the Jews—pointing out how many mistakes they are going to make if they don't wake up and get to Christ. Recently I received one of those full-of-paranoia, end-times pamphlets which proposed that the United Nations might some day move to Jerusalem. The Jews, it claimed, would welcome the Antichrist because of "the Zionist dream of ruling the world!" That is *not* the way to take the love of Christ to the Jews. I wish anti-Semitic Christians would stop and listen to what God has said. Referring to those who speak against the Jewish nation, He said, "I will . . . curse him that curseth thee" (Gen. 12:3).

I finally decided to begin with my "Blessings and Curses" talk, followed by "The Seven Feasts of Israel," and finally an explanation of "The Russian Invasion of Israel."

Blessings and Curses

A survey of Israel's blessings and curses throughout her long history shows what it means to be the people chosen by God. Israel has a destiny and the special attention of God. According to the relative reverence or irreverence of the Jewish people, so went the fortunes of the land of Israel.

Thus, when Abraham believed God and obeyed Him and set out for the Promised Land, wonderful promises were issued while he traveled that will remain in force forever. But when the Jews left the land in favor of the temporarily more fertile Egypt, they fell into slavery. Again, however, their faith began to prevail and they followed Moses. The Almighty delivered them out of Egypt but found their reverence wanting in the wilderness. A generation of apostates was replaced by a new generation of the faithful, and finally the chosen people retook the Promised Land.

And so it has gone—from golden calf to tabernacle and back, throughout Jewish history. Under the mighty sovereigns David and Solomon, Israel prospered; when north and south divided, Israel fell. The temple of God was destroyed by Nebuchadnezzar in

The Underground Church of Jerusalem

the sixth century before Christ, but Jewish pioneers, after seventy years of Babylonian captivity, rebuilt it.

Obviously the most grievous lack of faith on the part of Israel occurred when the Messiah came preaching the kingdom of God. A generation later the second temple was destroyed (A.D. 70), and when Roman paganism finished decimating Israel, Islam arrived.

Pagan religion in the Holy Land has always brought about tragedy and war. The coming of the Moslems heralded long-range problems for the Jews; we are just beginning to appreciate the gravity of those troubles even though that inconvenient Dome was put up in A.D. 691. The Crusaders, whose bloody work gave the Jews good reason to hate the cross forevermore, continued the curses. The age of the infamous Inquisition saw anti-Semitism reach sickening levels in Europe. The Jews were blamed for everything from sacrificing gentile children at Passover to underwriting the bubonic plague.

(Since few Jews came down with the plague, it was assumed they had poisoned certain wells in Europe and therefore they knew how to avoid the infection. Instead, the Jews were simply obeying their sensible public health laws: washing their hands before meals, not eating scavenger animals, and carefully sterilizing their kitchens. The Gentiles' lack of knowledge of the Old Testament was costly then as it is costly now.)

The Jew was regarded as so inferior to others during the age of the Reformation that even so steady a Bible-reader as Martin Luther cursed them (in his senility, it's fair to say). In England they had to wear the Star of David on their clothing so that all might readily identify these untouchables. They were not allowed to enter a Christian church! (How times changed since the days of the church of Jerusalem.) If a Jew did come to Christ, which happened occasionally despite everything, his money and his children were converted with him; the church simply took those things for its own. Spain solved the Jewish "problem" by deporting her entire Jewish population (and keeping their property). The Russians started their infamous pogroms, still very much in evidence in the twentieth century.

To say that all this anti-Semitism fulfilled prophecy is true (e.g. Deut. 28:64-66), but showing that this is true is not the recommended way to approach the Jew with the Scriptures. This survey simply shows the blessings and curses of being God's chosen people.

I decided to do this historical survey first, giving the listeners an overall picture of the biblical progress of Israel, while Mal developed the Abrahamic covenant. That way they could appreciate both God's choice of and interest in the Jewish people, and the progress of His special attentions. After Mal explained the legal covenants in the Old Testament, I discussed the seven feasts.

The Seven Feasts of Israel

The biblical account of the feasts God gave Israel (Lev. 23) gives opportunity for one of the best Bible studies I know. The church does not understand the meaning of these holy days, and so it has instituted others in their places. This is one of the ironic twists of non-biblical religion. What the Gentile misses here is vital.

The Underground Church of Jerusalem

A complete explanation of Passover and the other feasts is available in my book *Jesus, The Jew's Jew* (Creation House, 1973), but if one is willing to read Leviticus 23 in conjunction with the following chart, God will, as usual, reward the study.

FEAST	SYMBOL	FULFILLMENT
1. Passover	Blood	Salvation
2. Unleavened Bread	Body	Holiness
3. First Fruits*	New Life	Resurrection
4. Pentecost	Harvest	Holy Spirit
5. Trumpets	Deliverance	Rapture
6. Atonement	Repentance	Redemption
7. Tabernacles	Temple	Kingdom

It is not now my purpose to develop the exquisite symmetry of the feasts with the New Testament. But it is important to notice that they symbolically represent a schedule of spiritual affairs from creation to eternity. How beautifully God fulfills each one of these! How obedient Jesus was to His Father! He was crucified on Passover, buried on Unleavened Bread, raised on First Fruits; He sent the Holy Spirit on Pentecost and He will return for the church at the sound of the trumpet; Israel will atone at the second coming (". . . they shall look upon Me whom they pierced and they shall mourn for him . . ." Zech. 12:10) and all will have the kingdom when the Lord establishes His tabernacle on the earth. It's perfect, beautiful, and

*Known today as Easter.

useful. It is so like our God to give us gifts like the feasts.

Christians, I should say, are not required to celebrate the feasts; Jesus fulfilled each one for us. But since I would be talking to Jews, who have only the Old Covenant if they have any religion at all, the feasts seemed relevant. The Jews *do* have to celebrate each one if they are to keep the law and most of them attend to this requirement. I thought that if I explained how wonderfully Jesus brought each feast to its logical and spiritual conclusion they, best of all people, could appreciate that He was the Messiah.

The Book of Hebrews was designed for witnessing to the Jews, of course, but so many of its symbols and types are gone now. Today's Jew does not have a temple, sacrifices, nor a priesthood. He has forgotten that the blood is given for the remission of sin. Jesus' role as High Priest is not appreciated.

But the feasts are still here, in one form or another. And the Jews do know their feasts.

The Russian Invasion of Israel

I thought the Russian invasion should certainly seem relevant to the people who were going to withstand it some day. It is explained in full in Ezekiel 38–39, and the world political climate suggests that it is not so far off. Believe me, you can get an Israeli's undivided attention when you talk about what's going to happen to Israel!

The many details given by Ezekiel coordinate so well with the modern situation that biblical analysts were able to identify this invasion a century ago, before there was a restored Israel and before Russia became a world power capable of such an invasion. The old Scofield Reference Bible (1907), relying completely on Ezekiel, gives an accurate preview of this expected invasion. Such forewarning should be taken seriously today. Ezekiel's intricate forecast, complete with the names of the protagonists, was made 2,500 years in advance. Which of us would hazard to predict the political situation in the Middle East 2,500 years from *now*?

We were also presenting Mal's film "The Coming Russian Invasion of Israel," for which I wrote the script. I figured the Bible study on this would have a telling effect. This was very true, as it turned out.

Mal and I went to Israel to show God's chosen people the contemporary relevancy of the Book their forefathers had written. Later I will share the results of our efforts.

But first I want to tell you another reason for my going to Israel—I wanted to check on the progress of prophecy.

That may sound strange since some people don't even believe in Bible prophecy. But I find it necessary in my work to check up on it as time passes. I'm not merely convinced about the accuracy of prophecy; I actually want to watch it being fulfilled.

The major events of the Tribulation period, for which we ought to be watching, all take place in Israel. The end times will bring us the third temple, the Antichrist, and Armageddon.

So from time to time, I check up on Israeli plans to go ahead with the temple, to set up the situation which will bring the Antichrist and his treaty, and to watch for the ominous development of world war. Each time I go to Israel, things have progressed a little further.

The Temple

On the temple, things are at a standstill, at least where actual construction is concerned. The Moslems' Dome of the Rock is sitting on the temple site and that's all there is to that. An Israeli actually did apply for a building permit a few years ago in order to construct the temple of God, but it was rejected on the grounds that the site is not clear. This was done tongue-in-cheek, I suppose, but it did startle those who realize how much the temple has to do with the Tribulation times (2 Thess. 2:4 et al.).

So, construction of the temple cannot be accomplished as things stand, but there are other preparations necessary for establishing the temple of God, and these are well underway.

First, the prayer on the mount, mentioned earlier, is a spiritual exercise not noticed by the world since A.D. 70, the last time the temple stood. It should be appreciated that this is something new for our times, and it leads to reestablishing the site itself as holy Jewish ground. When the Israelis really do begin to think of the mount as the sacred site, there obviously will be that much more motivation to build the temple when it becomes possible.

Secondly, the Jerusalem Great Synagogue is now

under construction. This magnificent structure is designed to reestablish Jerusalem as the world center of Jewish worship. Think a moment—the Jews now worship wherever they happen to live, but this was never true in biblical times. Jerusalem was where God dwelt among His people, in the Most Holy Place, and Jerusalem was for worship. Sacrifices were only efficacious at Jerusalem and the priests only legally served at Jerusalem. One has only to experience with King Josiah the rage of God at the idea of the locally franchised temple at Bethel to appreciate that God will have Jerusalem as His holy city, for now and for always (2 Kings 23:15–20). The forgotten chapters of 2 Kings 22–24 comprise a miniature textbook on how not to worship God and how vital is His beloved Jerusalem.

The Great Synagogue is a stepping stone to the Tribulation temple and it will be the central shrine of world Judaism for a time. But it should not be confused with the future temple, as it has been by some prophecy analysts lately. The synagogue is not at all the equal of the temple in sanctity, magnitude, location, or purpose. But it does portend the reconstruction of God's house.

The Great Synagogue will be simply a house of worship, whereas the temple must be a "house of sacrifice" (2 Chron. 7:12). The Synagogue will accommodate some 1,500 worshipers—the mighty temples of Solomon and Herod provided for some three million over the duration of a high feast. The Synagogue will be simply a building, with a presiding rabbi, cantor, and choir, in keeping with present-day worship practices. The temples enjoyed a priesthood of hundreds, with duties far more relevant to the Jewish Law than today's mere services of praise. The temple was a five-level stone edifice covering thirty-four acres. The Great Synagogue and the temple of God are not comparable.

It is significant that the Jews of the world are financially contributing to this Great Synagogue; that in itself shows their very real interest in Jerusalem. After all, Jerusalem is a foreign city to the vast majority of Jewish people of the world today. It is not difficult to imagine that in some Jewish sectors little thought was ever given to Jerusalem. But the building of this synagogue has gotten them involved, and that's an important step toward the building of the temple.

Finally, I heard much more talk about the temple as a coming reality on this particular trip to Israel. In my previous tours, the temple was barely mentioned as a possibility, but now people are actually making jewelry for the women to wear to the temple and some are even composing music for the services. Archaeology has supplied many obscure facts about proper temple worship, and the common people, at least the worshiping common people, are learning about the future necessities. When it comes time to build, they will be ready!

The Antichrist

As to the Antichrist, I did not find him. Everybody always seems to be looking for him and accusing so many public figures of this heinous role in God's plan. But I was only looking for signs of his future appearance.

The Underground Church of Jerusalem

As usual, Israel is the place to look, but not because he's Jewish. I get so tired of people saying that the Antichrist is supposed to be a Jew. There is not the vaguest scriptural support for that belief. Read Daniel 11:37 in the Revised Standard, the NASB, the Living Bible, or almost any translation other than the King James and we can put the "God of his fathers" theory to rest. The King James translation was made during the golden age of anti-Semitism in England. This verse was so rendered seemingly to defame the Jews. (Notice that the King James substitutes "Easter" for "Passover" in Acts 12:4 as well. But I'm not on a crusade; it is still my favorite translation.) The tormentors of the Jews have always been Gentiles: Pharoah, Nebuchadnezzar, Antiochus, Titus, the Crusaders, the Inquisitors, Hitler, and Arafat.

So I wasn't looking for a Jew, but I was looking for a situation where the Jews may need somebody's help. The Antichrist's treaty will solve some political situation, and I was looking into politics for that. With the Lebanon-Syria situation and the latest Russian persecutions of Jews, I knew where to look.

He is to be a "man of peace," this smooth-talking future dictator. Daniel warns us astutely, ". . . and by peace [he] shall destroy many . . ." (Dan. 8:25). The Israelis have a terrible hunger for peace today and it's getting worse. Before my 1973 trip, the Israelis were very confident of their borders and their armed forces. They were not as likely to sue for peace before the Yom Kippur War because they felt they could hold off the Arabs forever. Had they not whipped the combined might of three nations in only six days in 1967? (The

Israelis quip, "Another day would have started a new week's rental on our tanks.")

But the War of October, 1973, was a rude awakening. The Israelis did not expect that attack, coming as it did on the Day of Atonement, the most sanctified Jewish holy day. Perhaps they trusted that the Arabs, in reality their cousins, would at least respect the fact that the Jewish people, even the soldiers, would be at worship and confession that day. But the Arabs demonstrated a new viciousness, attacking without regard for such fine points. Their cowardly assault was frighteningly successful.

Israel suffered in that short war. Every family in the land lost a boy and some lost all their sons. Peace was starting to become a necessity at almost any cost.

So recently, Israel has begun to sign peace accords, however tenuous. The "shuttle diplomacy" of former secretary of state Henry Kissinger found the Israelis willing to make deals, at least with lands in the Sinai. The precedent of an outsider coming in to make a peace covenant was established. The way things look now, the Israelis trust peace covenants, having successfully negotiated truces with Egypt and Syria since the 1973 war.

Things have become relatively quiet on the borders since the agreements were made and we now have something like an optimum climate for the Antichrist. We have Israel understandably eager for still more reassuring peace agreements and we have the Middle East as the focal point of a lot of negative global politics. The United Nations now has Israel on its daily agenda.

The Antichrist will presumably arrive on just such a scene, since he makes a seven-year peace covenant with Israel (Dan. 9:27). But his covenant will lead to world war, as the Scriptures lament. The Lord Himself shuddered, "For then shall be great tribulation, such as was not since the beginning of the world to this time, no, nor ever shall be. And except those days should be shortened, there should no flesh be saved . . ." (Matt. 24:21,22).

The situation with oil has made the whole Middle Eastern miasma come to a boil. The goings-on with Israel and the Arab oil suppliers have achieved world importance and the nations of the world fear another boycott of the precious black gold of the desert sands. It's very complicated at the moment; the Arabs always hint that the very presence of Israel in their midst upsets them so much that they may quit sending oil or may raise the price until the economy of the free world is crippled. Israel says the Jews are staying, nevertheless.

We are coming to that moment in prophecy where the whole world hates Israel. When that happens Israel will need protection, and lots of it. And that's what the Antichrist will offer.

They may not like him but they will have to listen to his offer. They will take what they can get at a time like that.

And we're coming to a time like that.

A Russian Invasion

Armageddon is preceded in prophecy by the Russian invasion of Israel. I asked a number of Israelis whether or not they think the Russians are coming. This was something I checked up on during my last two trips to Israel, before the Yom Kippur War and after. Before October, 1973, most Israelis laughed off my question. Why should Russia be concerned about Israel? Things were quiet with the Arabs, and Russia was far off and very detached from the Middle East and its local quibbling. But after the war the Israelis changed their tune considerably.

Frankly, they were worried after the Yom Kippur invasion by the Arabs. The world had been shown that Israel was vulnerable, at least to a point. The Arabs couldn't beat them, but they could fight them to a standstill. And who stepped in to get things stopped but Russia? Whose equipment were the Arabs using but Russia's? Who but the Russians trained the Arab troops?

The American forces in the area went on an "alert" status during those closing days of the 1973 War because there was a threat of Russian intervention. Fifty thousand Russian paratroops were mobilized in Yugoslavia, an informed Israeli told me, poised to attack to rescue the trapped Egyptians in the Sinai.

That did not happen; the Russians did not come. But for anyone who has read prophecy, it was a big step forward toward the Russian invasion.

Most people who follow foreign wars in newspapers do not realize who the combatants really are. A story came back from the Sinai about an overrun Egyptian missile base. When the Israelis surrounded it, a Russian commander presented himself. He spoke only Russian and the Israelis immediately sent for an interpreter. They were very interested in talking to this particular commander who was plying his trade so very far from home. An Israeli told me the story with pride because the punchline concerned the talent of the Israeli forces. The commander, it seemed, was overwhelmed with the difference between the Egyptian troops he led and the Israelis who routed them. "It took me six months to train my men in the use of our antiaircraft weaponry and you people storm in here and figure it all out in a few minutes!"

But the story has a serious point: the Russians are, in very real terms, *already* invading Israel. The presence of the Russian instructors and military advisors among the Arabs does not satisfy the prophecy, but it certainly leads toward it.

Russian persecution of the Jews in the USSR and its satellites is another sign of Russia's stance against Israel. This new level of anti-Semitism behind the Iron Curtain has seemed to come into being very recently. The Russians never liked Jews—who has?—but now they really are abusing them. The internal passports issued by the Communists have the designation "Jewish" in the case of Jewish-born natives. This is tantamount to the old star-on-the-coat mentality.

The Russians find it very inconvenient to have Jews among them because Jews do not make good robots. Historically, Jews never knuckled under to dictatorships and they have proved to be a very difficult people to oppress. They make awful Communists—they like personal freedom, they want to be allowed to be religious, and they never like being told what to do and how to live.

Well, lately the Jews have been trying to get out of Russia and they have been succeeding. World Jewry has put some effective pressure on the Kremlin and Jews have been leaving Russia with legal visas. They tend to go to America or Israel, bringing along all their industry and all their savvy.

That makes the Russians mad.

Nobody can get under your skin like a Jew. Love him and he gives it back double. Hate him and he will give it back double, too. The Russians have never learned to love the Jews and so they have problems with them. Spiritually speaking, one has to love God to love the Jews, and Russian leaders are usually not acquainted with God. Jesus loved His Father completely and He loved the Jews completely. But those who hate Jesus' Father hate the Jews, and that's how it has always been.

Also, Israel is in the way of Russian expansion into Africa and that also displeases the Communist overlords. Nothing would be more convenient for the progress of Russian world domination than for the Israelis to get out of the way. The road to Angola and the rest of troubled Africa goes through the Middle East. And while Russia has been able to cultivate friendships of a sort with the Arabs, they certainly have no love affair with Israel.

It would be better for Russia if she could chase out the Jews and put a Russian base in Israel. Then Russia's navy would have fine ports on the Mediterranean and their airplanes could have facilities close to the African continent. Israel is so well developed that Russian industry and commerce would enjoy a fine climate, as in Eastern Europe. When the Russians took over in East Germany, it was with appreciation of what the industrious Germans had accomplished with the territory; they didn't tear it down, they just

The Underground Church of Jerusalem

hoisted a Russian flag over the factories and kept it all moving along for the glory of communism.

What a plum Israel would make for Russia!

Don't think for a moment that the Israelis don't know it. On *this* trip people in Israel were thinking Russian! They have no delusions about their enemy from the north. They may not comprehend a lot of prophecy, but they know who their enemies are. You can depend on it; Israel sees Red.

I was told in Israel before the 1973 War, "Why worry about Russia? Relax. They don't even think about us." After the war it changed to "Yes, they're dangerous, but the United States will protect us. We're watching out for the Communists, but we feel secure."

But on this last trip it was more like, "What if the Russians come? Can we depend on the United States? What will we do?" Some knowledgeable people in Israel are beginning to think of America as a fair-weather friend. When the oil spigot gets turned down, will the Americans still side with Israel or will they go where the oil is?

Some American oil executives, in a mealy-mouthed display of modern anti-Semitism, have begun to talk about what great friends of ours the Arabs are. The incredible idea that the Americans and the Arabs have close ties going back into history has been suggested by these money-hungry turncoats who inevitably side with the greater profit margin in any conflict.

Can Israel depend on us in the Western world if Russia invades?

"I will bless them that bless thee!"

5.
Now You See It...
The Visible Church

I should say a word for the Italians. After all, it was they who finally got Mal and me to Israel.

It happened that our particular tour was bumped from a crowded El Al flight to Italy's Alitalia Airlines, which also serves Ben Gurion Airport in Tel Aviv. Flying at tour prices, Mal and I had to take what we could get, and we looked forward to Italian food on our substitute flight.

That was not to be. At the wishes—or rather at the ultimatum—of the orthodox Jewish passengers who were bumped along with us, kosher food was served throughout the crossing by the Italian crew: El Al had catered our flight!

The dietary laws of the Old Testament are considered mandatory by the orthodox Jews. One extreme practice is the nearly fanatic separation of milk and meat dishes, which is not actually scriptural. Exodus 23:19 commands the Jewish people not to boil "the kid in its mother's milk," a disgusting rite practiced by pagans, but this is the only hint of such a distinction

The Underground Church of Jerusalem

in the Bible. But the Jews have long built hedges around the law and this is one of the outlying hedges. Some American Jewish kitchens have two dishwashers in order to keep separate the dishes used for milk from those used for meat. Neither can the dishes used for milk be in the sink with dishes used for meat. There is separate storage of the dishes in the cupboards as well.

Counting the Passover dishes, which are different from those used year-round, the proper orthodox Jewish woman maintains four separate sets of dishes and silverware.

There are two separate kitchens on every El Al airliner, in keeping with the preferences of highly religious passengers. All food served by El Al conforms to the strictest orthodox requirements, as it did on our Alitalia flight.

When one sees those prayerful ones get up and walk to the front of the airplane to pray in flight (the front when traveling toward Israel, the rear when returning—the orthodox always face the east, representing the position of the temple, when praying) one realizes that the plane ride itself is a religious rite.

Our Italian crew was very patient and courteous, asking each passenger if he wished to have the kosher food. Mal and I acquiesced, receiving trays covered with plastic bubbles containing separate plastic-wrapped dishes within. No gentile hands had touched that food!

But the Alitalia folks had their gentile hands full with their complement of Jewish tourists off to Israel. Italians themselves are known for getting excited, but one has to travel with the chosen people to the Prom-

Now You See It . . . The Visible Church

ised Land to see *real* excitement. And besides, Jews make dangerous passengers these days. That famous hijacking and subsequent rescue at Entebbe had happened to an Air France plane mainly because many of the passengers were Jewish and the flight had originated in Israel. Mal and I speculated that we might be taken off to some barbaric land and have to make the best of things until the Israeli army landed.

Indeed, when we had to change planes at Rome (at 4:30 A.M. after a long night of trying to speak Italian) we were made very jumpy by the security precautions. The Rome airport personnel were not particularly happy to see us arrive.

During the layover, we were watched by black-haired young men with machine guns who looked like they had stepped right out of *The Godfather*. We were made to clear a TV-scanner security check even though we had just gotten off an Alitalia airplane. Did they think we had somehow acquired hijacking hardware in flight? No, they were just taking the normal care with people who insist on traveling to and from the Holy Land. The terrorists have made their point.

On the whole the Italians did a good job with the flights and we arrived on time. There really hasn't been much bad blood between Italians and Jews now that the Jews have survived the Roman Empire and World War II. We were handled gingerly, though, like fragile packages.

I missed the playing of "Avenu Shalom Aleichem," the magnificent Israeli song of welcome sounded through the speakers of the El Al planes when God's land is sighted. But I was thunderstruck as usual with the sheer beauty of the fertile Tel Aviv-Jaffa terrain as we cleared the Mediterranean and made preparations to land. God picked a lovely place for His headquarters on earth.

It was 9:00 A.M. our time—three in the afternoon in Israel—when we started through the intricate security procedures for disembarking at Ben Gurion. Being preoccupied with my need for sleep, I somehow left the film copy I was carrying of "The Coming Russian Invasion of Israel" on the little bus that took us from the plane to the terminal. I knew it would be an attention-getter when I reclaimed it, and it was. "Shulchan?" "Yours?" asked the security man who had retrieved it from the bus. He was incredulous and that spat-out *"shulchan?"* said worlds of things. "You look Jewish to me," he might have gone on to say. "Why do you walk around with tripe like this? Why bring it *here?*" He walked away shaking his head.

In disembarking, and later in going home through the El Al security, everyone seemed to find it interesting that I had that film, a two-testament Bible, and a gentile friend with me. With my beard and patently Jewish face, I looked more the part of a returning native than an American Bible teacher, and people always spoke to me first in Hebrew.

Another occupational hazard of mine—that I speak up for Christ loud and clear in Hebrew and English—is more serious, as we will now see when we look at the visible church in Israel. The church was the first place Mal and I went while observing that lovely first day of rest and there was a lot to see, as I indicated

Now You See It . . . The Visible Church

earlier. The visible church is as complex as the underground church.

We unpacked in Jerusalem and found our way to Mal's favorite restaurant, which specializes in classy French cuisine, near Zion Square. But the quality of the food had deteriorated, we noticed, since our last meal there and the boss tried to cheat us on the check. (We had seven dollars change coming and he tried to give Mal seven Israeli pounds instead. I caught the shift of currencies, though, and whispered to Mal that the Israeli pounds were worth only about twelve cents each.)

I spent the first night at the Shalom Hotel and Mal went to his room at the YMCA. I moved to a friend's apartment the second night, but on that first night after being awake for forty straight hours, I wasn't up to reminiscing with a buddy. I wanted to *sleep!* It was money well spent.

There was nothing to read in my room except the tourist booklets, so I opened one of them and glanced through it. It advertised the land competently and provided tourist tips on what to see and where to go. One passage, designed to help tourists with the shopping hours in Jerusalem, is worth quoting in its entirety:

> Shopping hours in Jerusalem, East, West, and Old, vary. Most stores open around 8.30 or 9 a.m., close for lunch 1 p.m. to 2, 3 or 4 p.m., and remain open to around 7 p.m. Some shops don't close for lunch at all. Most West Jerusalem stores close Tuesday and Friday afternoons, and of course, on the Sabbath. Old City and other East Jerusalem shops don't usually take full afternoons off in

mid-week. They also stay open on Saturdays, remaining closed on either Fridays or Sundays, depending whether the owner is of the Moslem or Christian faith.

That ought to clear things up for shoppers.

Now let's face it. You just don't find that kind of literature anywhere else. That's distinctly Israel.

I had to combine with the above information the fact that some Jewish stores take half-holidays every day during the Feast of Tabernacles, depending, presumably, on the piety of the owner. Also, it might be mentioned, the fancy shops in the lower promenade of the plush King David Hotel remain open late in the evening, should tourists need a mink coat, a diamond, or the like.

I did quite a bit of shopping. For my son, I bought a T-shirt with "Coca-Cola" in Hebrew along the front and for my wife a fancy dress and a bottle of *Mazeltov,* "the perfume that brings good luck." All of the shopping was harrowing, with high prices and non-English-speaking merchants. I would approach, carefully enunciating, *"Atah dabahr Anglit?"* and the storekeeper would wince at my accent and say brokenly, "Try . . . it . . . in . . . English."

One morning I set out to buy fruit drinks for our training-lecture class in which Mal attempted to disciple those interested in teaching the "Walk Through the Bible" seminar after we left. The merchant, in this case, spoke Rumanian only. Stand before your mirror and try to say, "Do you have straws?" in Rumanian. Try to pantomime what a straw is. Try to transfer the value in dollars and cents to pounds and *agarot* (one-hundred *agarot* in a pound) while somebody grabs

Now You See It . . . The Visible Church

your fistful of cash and numbers it all in a language foreign to your ears.

Please don't be discouraged. Try to go to Israel anyway.

Reading further in my tourist book, I found the recommendation to see the tombs of the prophets under the heading, "What's New in Jerusalem?" A friend and I laughed until we cried over the idea that the 3,000-year-old monuments were "new." My friend had pictured the newsroom where the tourist book is made up: "Have you got the copy ready, Eliezer?" "Sure, chief!" "What's new this week?" "The tombs of the prophets!"

I saw our own ads, inviting the public and the tourists to attend our Bible study at the YMCA. A missionary assistant had placed these ads for Mal before we arrived. I wondered if we would get a roomful of cynical tourists.

As I closed the book my sleepy eyes fell on the cover and I saw an amazing demonstration of building a hedge around the law. The cover was a reproduction of a magnificent painting by a rabbi, and all the people in the painting were made either of steel parts or parts of insects. There was a horrible bug-faced soldier struggling with a robot-like opponent in the center. The prohibition against the Jews making graven images was extended in the past to not representing the human figure even in paint, but this rabbi had found a solution.

Christian Worship in Public View

I have already alluded to the interesting and spiritually rejuvenating churches Mal and I attended that

The Underground Church of Jerusalem

first Sabbath (Saturday) morning. Both the deeply earnest and grave atmosphere of the Messianic Assembly and the joyful sermon on the Feast of Tabernacles we heard at the Baptist House gave insight to the ways and mission of the church in Israel.

Worth mentioning is a third church we attended later in the week where a baptism was held under the floor! The candidate came forward in a white gown and the minister received him, explaining the procedure of baptism first in Hebrew, then in English. Then men who were presumably deacons went forward, lifted the rug from the podium, and began to take up the floor, board by board. The floorboards were not nailed down, but were loose for this very purpose.

Under the floor was a pool of water deep enough for the immersion. Our new brother was washed and prayed for there beneath the podium as we all exulted.

Now I could not quite figure out the reason for that system. The church may have simply wanted to remove the baptistry from where it might offend the unsaved Jews who occasionally come into the services (though purification by washing is a thoroughly Jewish concept practiced even at the Passover table today). Baptism is not against any law in Israel and people are baptized regularly in the Jordan River, as I myself was on a previous trip. But the little church still practiced this unusual way of doing it. Perhaps it more resembled the way the Jews themselves used to bathe before entering the temple walls, in the *mikva'ot*, or ritual baths. Some orthodox synagogues have *mikva'ot* here in America and they use them, for one thing, to "baptize" or purify converts to Judaism.

Now You See It . . . The Visible Church

They are invariably pools in the floor of special rooms, rather than being on display in the sanctuary wall, as in many Baptist churches in America.

In any case, the purpose was not to hide the baptistry. This was an open church in downtown Jerusalem, one of the "visible" churches of the Holy Land. They vary in nature and purpose (and witness) but they are open to the scrutiny of the Jews. Unlike the underground church, the visible congregations conduct Christianity in public.

Christian Settlements

Some of the visible churches take the form of "settlements," in keeping with the Israeli way of doing things. Not unlike the *kibbutzim,* they are cooperative organizations usually concerned with cultivating the land or otherwise producing goods for, and improving, Israel. They are non-evangelistic in character, approved by the government and their neighbors, and in general provide a reasonably good testimony for the true church.

Nes Amim (Miracle of the Nations) is one of them. It was founded in Galilee in 1962 as a settlement for European Protestants, and its business is to plant the land and love the Jews. It was originally established under a cloud of suspicion by the orthodox, who saw it as a potential base of operations for missionary work. It was ultimately necessary for each candidate for membership in the community to sign an affidavit to the effect that he had no missionary purpose in Israel but only sought to support and build the land. A supervisory committee was set up to constantly check

The Underground Church of Jerusalem

on the activities at *Nes Amim* and it was agreed that no converted Jew would ever reside there.

No German was ever to reside there either, by the request of the neighboring *Kibbutz Lohamei Hagetaot*, founded by survivors of the Warsaw Ghetto.

Ninety people—fifteen couples and their children—make up the population of prosperous *Nes Amim* today, and the little group is helping to fulfill one of Isaiah's most welcome and stunning prophecies—"The desert shall . . . blossom as the rose" (Isa. 35:1). *Nes Amim* exports beautiful greenhouse roses every winter. Young visitors put in temporary stints at the unique settlement—the Dutch government allows the substitution of *Nes Amim* work for military service. The youngsters are strong Christians deeply devoted to the Holy Land.

The members work six days, resting and worshiping on Saturdays, light Chanukah candles, and trim Christmas trees.

The wise and theologically sound young minister of this *moshav* (colony, distinguished from a *kibbutz* by its communal, rather than simply collective, atmosphere) stated that the founding of the Jewish state in 1948 came as "a shock to Christian theology. It caused us to reevaluate and redefine what the church has believed throughout the ages—that God had forsaken the Jews when they rejected the Messiah."[*]

Part of the reevaluation program at this *moshav* is the extension of Christian industry and love toward

---

[*]Quotations and some factual information in this section from the article, "Israeli Settlements with Christmas Trees," by Joan Borstin; *Jewish Digest*, Dec. 1976, p. 37. Reprinted from *Hadassah* magazine (Vol. 57, No. 4).

the Jews, a holy and advisable way to handle God's own.

It is a testimony to the patience and kindness of the *Nes Amim* pioneers that their neighbors have accepted them to the degree that a German family responsible for saving many Jewish lives during the Holocaust was ultimately permitted to reside at the settlement. This opened the way for young German Christians to put in volunteer stints. "Love covers a multitude of sins" (1 Pet. 4:8, RSV*).

Nes Amim is initiating a Christian-Jewish dialogue center, where rabbis and Christian theologians will speak. The idea is to turn the Christian church toward a greater understanding of the Jew; Christians who visit *Nes Amim* come away with quite a new perspective on this vital spiritual issue. In accordance with their promise to Israel, they may not do direct missionary work at *Nes Amim*, but they make a great difference for the Lord.

Cut in the same mold as *Nes Amim* is another European Christian *moshav*, *Yad Hashmona* (Monument to the Eight) founded by Finnish Christians. It was established in memory of eight Finnish Jews who were handed over to the Gestapo by the government of Finland during World War II.

Yad Hasmona produces beautiful furniture in its carpentry shop but its major purpose and income is tourism. It seeks, not unlike *Nes Amim*, to promote a Christian testimony through example rather than direct witness to the Jews, and it gets good results in this

---

*From the Revised Standard Version of the Bible, copyrighted 1946, 1952, © 1971, 1973.

way. A lady who belonged to American-founded *Moshav Neve Ilan*, a neighboring Israeli settlement, commented, "At first I was worried about living so close to Christians. I had, after all, come 6,000 miles [from America] to insure the Jewishness of my children. Happily, my fears were unfounded, and my early negative attitudes have reversed themselves. They are very nice people, committed to working their land, and very uninterested in converting anyone."

Now actually, it would be to the spiritual discredit of such Christian settlements if they were "very uninterested" in bringing the Jews to Christ. This would not be an appropriate response to the admonitions of the New Testament at all. It is just that their ministries must take a different form, due to the agreement that had to be made for the original establishment of the *moshavim*. They are not supposed to evangelize, so they don't. But a Jewish reaction like "They are very nice people" is quite an accomplishment. My father did not believe Christians were "very nice people"; he thought they were murderers. People carrying crosses on Good Friday murdered the Jews in Latvia where my father was brought up. I'm missing some uncles and aunts because of people who *said* they were Christians and who *said* they were killing people in the name of Christ. My father always felt it safer to avoid all Gentiles and had little interest in Christian doctrine. He died after a lifetime of seventy years during which the only "gospel" he ever heard came from the barrel of a rifle.

So for the Jews to see Christians as nice people at least makes up for some of the poor groundwork laid in the past. If the Christians who hate Jews today would only see what their hatred does to any future Christian witness, they might keep their bigotry to themselves—or hopefully get rid of this miserable sin. The cause of Christ is not helped much by the persecution of His brothers.

There is a Christian commune near Tel Aviv which I can happily say is witnessing strongly, one-on-one, in the streets of Israel and gathering a harvest. There are settlements behind the scenes where Christians are testifying with the fearlessness of Peter at Pentecost. And they're occasionally losing their visas and getting sent home.

Missions to the Arabs

There are settlements throughout the land that witness to the Arabs. This part of the visible church is allowed free operation, of course, and the Israelis have grown to appreciate what happens to an Arab when he becomes a genuine Christian.

The Arab "Christians" who took part in the bloody Lebanese civil war represented to most Jews of the world the familiar Christian-killer figure, but the Israelis, shrewder judges of the Middle-Eastern character, have seen that true Christianity quiets Arab belligerence. Too bad the American Christian church does not impress the Jews here as much as the Israeli Christian church impresses the Jews there. Even though we have taken the gospel throughout the world we have all but ignored our own Jewish population, and we have certainly not made them jealous as Paul admonished us to do (Rom. 11:11).

The Underground Church of Jerusalem

The Baptist Village is one of the Arab ministries in Israel. This is an American settlement of the rather liberal American Baptist denomination. The Baptists operate four open churches in Jerusalem, Acre, and Nazareth, as well as schools and youth centers, all aimed at the Arabs. "We don't think leading Jews to Jesus is a negative thing," one of the Baptist officials condescended to say, and the Baptist Village does accept Jewish converts for residence, to mild government disapproval. Perhaps the government has decided that putting up with the conversions of a few misled Jews is not a bad price for the soothing work of the denomination among the sometimes dangerous Israeli Arabs. The rabbis don't like the idea, to say the least, but the World Baptist Church generally supports Israel, and Baptists comprise the second largest tourist group after the Jews themselves.

The Jewish estimation of a ministry like the Baptist Village is positive. An excerpt from an article in a Jewish periodical illustrates this attitude:

> Despite their willingness to serve as "witnesses to the truth about Jesus," which would make many suspicious and uneasy, they have been careful to avoid approaches offensive to Jews and Moslems, and are generally respected by Israeli Government and political leaders. They have been loyal citizens of the country since its inception, and have made a genuine effort to hasten the process of peaceful integration between the Israeli Jew, Christian, and Moslem.*

*See footnote on page 74.

Now You See It . . . The Visible Church

When Paul spoke to the intellectuals at Athens he did not expect many converts, but he impressed them to see Christianity in a better light. The Lord Himself addressed hostile crowds without expecting a harvest because He knew the hearts of men. Our faith has always needed some good public relations work to support the main thrust of testimony. "Unto the Jews I became as a Jew . . ." (1 Cor. 9:20).

Perhaps the establishment of a sound reputation in the eyes of the secular nation is necessary to a potent witness. These visible churches have impressed the Jews of Israel favorably and their members are much more likely to get a hearing in a Christian-Jewish dialogue than American Christians who do so little for the Jews. Nicodemus approached Jesus because the Messiah was already certified as "a teacher come from God" in his eyes. He came by night, knowing that Jesus' witnessing ministry was always threatened (and because he likely did not want to be seen by his peers). But he *came.* And he asked about salvation.

It is possible that there are numbers of Nicodemus' descendants in Israel today who want to talk to a Christian. They might come by stealth, but they will come, and they will come to Christians who love the land and love the Jews. The visible church may not be holding evangelistic services in stadiums, but they do promote a good witness and behind the scenes some Jews are saved.

The government and the orthodox Jews know that some Jews are being saved; otherwise they would not have those rules about Jewish converts residing on the *moshavim*. Both sides of the spiritual conflict measure their every move with a view to human relations. That is just the nature of Israel.

Now, are the Christians who agree not to witness being weak? Are they really the true servants of Christ if they keep their witness "incognito"?

There is certainly biblical sanction for tact in witnessing. When the shoe was on the other foot—when the Jews went to the Gentiles, whom they expected to find hostile to the gospel, they did so very diplomatically when the occasion called. Consider the lesson of master-missionary Paul in his discussions about witnessing: "To the weak became I as weak, that I might gain the weak: I am made all things to all men, that I might by all means save some" (1 Cor. 9:22).

Paul was never really "weak" when we consider the massive success of his ministry, but he allowed for the peculiarities of the various societies he served. Being free from the Jewish law he still acted as a Jew for the Jews' sake; though liberated from the bonds of pagan philosophy, he still was a Greek to the Greeks. And he did it all "for the gospel's sake" (1 Cor. 9:23).

The pledge not to witness exacted by the Israeli government is aimed at avoiding open conflict over Christianity in the Holy Land. The government is not so misinformed about the true church that they think the Christians will never speak of Christ. They know there will be testimony given and received in Israel about the Galilean. But they do want to avoid street meetings, public discussions, and anything that smacks of any sort of "crusade." The pledge sort of keeps things in proper proportion.

Now You See It . . . The Visible Church

This brings up the interesting idea that people under an admonition *not* to do something tend to do it all the more. If the Israeli government were to make a *law* against witnessing, they well know that the witnessing would double and triple. The Russians have been smart enough not to outlaw Christianity—they just make it very inconvenient, we might say. The Israelis have found it expedient to voice their views against the practice and go no further. It's perhaps the best of all possible moves on their part.

We might consider the witnessing to the Jew in America compared with that in Israel. Over here where any Christian may witness to anyone he likes, the Jews generally get left out. But in Israel, where Christian residents have had to make an informal pledge not to aggressively promote the gospel, the chosen people are seeing, hearing, and often believing the testimony of the true church. Interesting.

Christian Institutions

We should not leave the subject of the visible church in Israel without citing the effects of the Christian training institutions in the land. They are a part of the church, and usually the part the Israelis see the most. The American Institute of Holy Land Studies, for example, is located on Mount Zion in Jerusalem, next to the temple site. There, young American seminarians go in and out of classes in plain view of the holiest of the orthodox community.

The Institute is thoroughly biblical and evangelical, but it makes a point of not witnessing in favor of training its student body in Jewish custom and tradition. Graduates come out as superior witnesses to Jewish people, usually returning to the United States and assisting with Jewish evangelism here. They often found churches which then have a real appreciation for the Holy Land and the chosen people. Again, it is a government agreement which holds back the witnessing, but the government cannot hold back the dispensing of knowledge which later on contributes to witnessing.

The land is well populated with such schools, particularly of the monastery variety, and they continually dispense a kind of knowledge and history that is practically unknown in the United States. Our history textbooks tend to begin Western civilization with ancient Greece or Rome, skipping over ancient Israel with its rich and varied culture and its monumental spiritual contributions. Israel is twice as old as Rome, reaching back to 2,000 B.C., and its laws and social customs deeply affect every part of our society today. But we all grow up over here thinking we owe our culture to the pagans instead.

In truth, this affects our churches as well. We tend to read the New Testament, which was written during the Roman age, to the exclusion of the Old. We sometimes think the apostles used the New Testament in their teaching, when actually they never saw one. When Paul taught the Scriptures, he taught the Old Testament. When the New Testament praises the Scriptures in respect to their being good for doctrine, correction, and reproof, it refers exclusively to the Old Testament, the only Bible in circulation when the Epistles were written. When Jesus said, "It is written," He certainly meant that it is written in the Old

Now You See It . . . The Visible Church

Testament. Jesus was an Old Testament scholar and he quoted only from it. The churches of Asia read only the Old Testament and the hundreds of epistles that came to them. Those churches were founded on the Old Testament just as our government was founded on what were initially Jewish principles.

The Holy Land institutions bring out these facts and they give Christians studying there a new perspective on what their faith is all about. A Christian who knows Israel and knows the Old Testament is a knowledgeable Christian with a depth to his faith not received any other way. On the other hand, a wholly American-trained Christian thinks of Christianity as more a system of behavior, since his main learning has been in the New Testament, and particularly in the Epistles. Most of America's Christian Bible classes emphasize the study of ten percent of the Bible ninety percent of the time.

And so, when I am called to speak at a seminary, the Bible students and their professors are as intrigued with my "secret understanding" as are the good folk of the churches. Here is my "secret"—study Israel and the Jews. You'll find God there.

I can't resist giving an example. Jesus blessed the bread and the wine at the Passover table (Matt. 26:26–27). After He did so He made statements about their spiritual meaning: "This is my body . . . This is my blood." But what did He say in the actual blessings? With what words did He bless those foods? What are the Jewish blessings over bread and wine? Do they say anything relevant to Christians?

As a matter of fact they do.

And I'm probably safe in saying that you don't

know those blessings. Don't feel embarrassed; no one at your local seminary knows them either. Neither does your pastor. They are virtually unknown to Christians, and yet in them is contained the exquisite beauty and total fulfillment of Communion.

Who knows those blessings?

Any Jew.

Find one and ask him. You'll be glad you did.

The blessings aren't printed in the gospel and you may wonder why. The answer is easy; the gospel was never meant for a wholly gentile church. There was never supposed to be any such thing. Matthew didn't have to write out Jewish blessings for Jews. You need a Jew—you could put up with at least *one*—in your church to explain this part of the gospel to you. And there are other parts of the New Testament that only the Jew can make clear, believe me. The New Testament is a Jewish Book.

You could also ask a gentile Christian *trained in Israel*. No doubt he'll know those blessings and a lot more besides. So credit those Christian institutions of the Holy Land. They're doing a vital job.

I'll translate those blessings for you, but that does not mean you should continue to ignore the Jews. Find one and ask him something else. Ask him if he will be your friend, even after all that has happened.

Jesus blessed the bread this way:

> Blessed art Thou, O Lord our God, King of the universe, *Who bringest forth bread from the earth* (italics mine).

Then He said, "This bread is my body."

The symbolism is clear. His body was to be brought

forth from the earth that very week, and His astonished disciples were to see an amazing fulfillment of that simple blessing they had said all their lives. It had been said exactly that way from time immemorial, but now it found its greater meaning in Christ.

Over the wine, Jesus said:

> Blessed art Thou, O Lord our God, King of the universe, *Creator of the fruit of the vine* (italics mine).

He had told them previously, "I am the true vine." Those early church members, the disciples, were the branches. And *we* are their fruit. Jesus was thanking God for *us,* the ultimate fruit of the vine. The Jewish bridegroom always drank a cup with his bride at the time their covenant was signed and the price for the bride was paid (the cross). Then he would tell her, "I go to prepare a place for you," return to his father's house, and then come back for her later with a shout.

Christian Tourists

Finally we should give credit to the most massive visible Christian church in the history of Israel, having tens of thousands of members and walking the streets of every city and hamlet in the Promised Land day and night. I refer to the Christian tourists.

An ever-shifting group, they come in droves, in never-ending plane loads, from almost every nation of the world, and they are the cream of the Christian crop. They are the Bible readers who have discovered that their Bible concerns Israel throughout, and they want to see the land for themselves. They are a tre-

The Underground Church of Jerusalem

mendous witness to the Israelis, who at least appreciate having their business, if not their faith. God has arranged this Christian tithe to Israel and is sending the Gentiles back to the Jews.

The Israelis watch the tourists very carefully. More often than not, they see real devotion to the land. They see religious consecration of a kind not seen at the Wailing Wall—people willing to come thousands of miles to what is an alien land in order to see traces of the Savior who walked there. They see prayer and dedication. They see godly Christians.

Probably those tourists do more to influence the Israelis that Christianity is real and vital than the small number of visible Christians within the land. If the least you can do for the Jews is go to Israel, then go to Israel.

6.
Now You Don't...
The Underground Church

In Israel the invisible church is much more interesting than the visible. What happens underground over there, as I indicated earlier, is truly inspiring.

It started practically at Pentecost, this underground church, and it flourishes today for those who know where to look and who might be accepted into the ranks. These people will surely inherit the earth, along with the meek.

Covert worship of Jesus in Israel has a long and distinguished history. The Lord has been worshiped in spite of hordes of pagans of every stripe and in spite of uncomprehending Jewish legalists.

I looked at an archaeological find on this past trip that, for me, ranks with the best of them. The diggers have unearthed three *mikva'ot*, ritual baths, right by the southern wall of the temple site on the western end. There they sit, seeing the sunlight for the first time since Titus, I suppose, and they have a grand significance. They well may have been involved in the very first act of the underground church of Jerusalem.

The Underground Church of Jerusalem

The western end of the southern wall was once the site of the Huldah Gate, where the common folk came into the temple. Jesus and His men were among those field workers and tradesmen who went in by this "service entrance," and no doubt they washed in the *mikva'ot*. They are on ground level, in keeping with the purpose of washing for purification.

The rich folks entered by the more convenient Eastern or Golden Gate which faced the Mount of Olives on the east side of the sanctuary, and they probably came clean already—in fact, they probably looked as gorgeous as those orthodox of the *Mea Shearim* do today.

The Eastern Gate is closed now, but it will open for the King when He comes.

What's the significance of all this? Well, those newly discovered *mikva'ot* lie directly below Solomon's Portico up on the summit level. Many biblical scholars hold that the miracle of Pentecost happened there in the Portico, and this makes sense. Peter and company would more likely have been found up there with the plain folks than over at the sanctuary or the Eastern Gate, particularly in the morning when people were arriving.

When the Holy Spirit came and the 3,000 were saved, Peter called for their baptism (Acts 2:38–41). It's speculation, but now that the *mikva'ot* have been found we have a reasonable place for that massive baptismal ceremony. The baptism of the 3,000 has always been a problem to scholars since there is not much water around Jerusalem. Such a large group certainly would not have gone up to the sanctuary area, and the various small pools outside the temple

Now You Don't . . . The Underground Church

(e.g. Siloam) would have been very inefficient for such numbers. It is not likely they would have gone all the way to the Jordan when they had only just arrived for the feast.

So, maybe they want to the *mikva'ot* right down the hill. The baths were designed for crowds; they were large and steadily refilled with fresh water. Peter could have said, as he led the new believers out the Huldah Gate, "Now let's really be purified."

If that happened, it was the first "underground" act of the church. It would have been unthinkable to go deeper into the temple area for water since baptism was not looked upon very kindly in Jerusalem at that point. Pilate had washed his hands of Jesus only seven weeks before and the controversy that must have existed over the missing body had people edgy. Peter probably wanted to avoid any trouble with officials, but down at the *mikva'ot* it was perfectly appropriate for a large number of people to get into the water.

So perhaps the 3,000 were discreetly washed in the *mikva'ot* and the underground church got underway. From the looks of that concealed baptistry under the floor of the church that Mal and I saw, things haven't changed much over the years.

Of course, when Peter and John came by and healed the beggar later on (Acts 3), everybody was in on it. And we can understand from the results of that miracle why Peter would have exercised discretion back at Pentecost; the security people came by ("the captain of the temple"), "And they laid hands on them and put them in hold unto the next day . . ." (Acts 4:3). The police were too late, of course. While Peter and

The Underground Church of Jerusalem

John spent the night in the cooler, 5,000 people were accepted into the underground church of Jerusalem (Acts 4:4).

But that underground church probably didn't last. Obviously, the Jewish Christians, along with all the rest of the Israelites, were vanquished by the Romans in the siege and temple destruction of A.D. 70. One's particular messianic beliefs were not of much consequence when Titus and his legions conducted their murderous assault. Israel was ruined, church and temple alike, in a final battle that established a casualty rate that has never been equaled in any single battle! More than one million people were slaughtered in five months' time.

And so we find that the church of Jerusalem is not mentioned in Revelation 1–4, where the Lord reviews the actions of the various established churches late in the first century. Of course, the church of Rome is not mentioned either, but we can follow its actions through secular history; it progressed mightily, finally overwhelming the Roman Empire itself. It lost sanctification along the way, but it prevailed.

But in the Holy City everything came to a terrible standstill. Now we can assume there were hearty souls who refused to leave God's chosen place regardless of the conditions for staying and who probably continued to worship on the empty, leveled summit. They have always been there. But the once-mighty Christian church has never risen again in Jerusalem.

Undoubtedly true Christians could be found throughout the land by those who knew where to find them, and their presence was known in the age of Hadrian (A.D. 135) who built a pagan temple on the holy mount. The deeply anti-Semitic Roman Emperor Hadrian thought this would be the final solution to the Jewish problem—wipe out their holy site and their religion would disappear. He forebade observance of the Jewish law and persecuted the chosen people tirelessly, running up more of those breathtaking casualty figures in Israel. The false messiah Bar Kochba tried to lead a revolt against Rome, but it was hopeless. This time the Romans almost did find the final solution—the Jews dispersed so widely that they never really occupied the land again until 1948.

But the Christians were there, even during the bloody times of Hadrian, quietly testifying that all this destruction showed God's wrath against those who rejected the Messiah. Jews were saved back then and found peace even in those horrible ages of dispersion.

The church remained underground through the coming of the Moslems, and they watched as the holy site was desecrated yet again with the construction of the Dome of the Rock. They awaited the Lord through hopeless centuries of Middle-Eastern paganism. We fail to appreciate their faithfulness in keeping the light on in Jerusalem and steadily testifying of the Lord to all who would listen. We know they were there because the Crusaders found them there when they arrived at the beginning of this millennium.

But the Crusaders provided little relief to the underground church in Israel. Like the plundering Romans, they killed and butchered indiscriminately—Jews, Moslems, Christians—whoever seemed to be in the way of "liberating and cleansing" the Holy Land. The true church was now obliged to hide from the

The Underground Church of Jerusalem

Crusaders, as they had hidden from the Moslems, the Romans, and the Jews before them.

The Crusaders captured the Dome for a time and placed a cross on the top. They thought they had Solomon's original temple, which speaks of their lack of Old Testament knowledge.

The church of Rome now dominated the Christian world, virtually copyrighted the Bible for private use, dispensed all knowledge, forgave sins (or didn't forgive sins), and provided certification to the saved at its discretion. This drove the true church ever further underground. Those in real communication with the Lord could no more participate in this church than they could have been loyal to Rome in the first century. Rather, like the Jews, they had to remain out of sight to avoid real persecution.

Like the Jews too, they were caught occasionally. The Inquisition saw the torture and murder of believing Christians as well as Jews and pagans; those who would not subscribe to the religion of Rome were the enemy to the overlords of the state. The love of Christ went so far underground that it was rarely spoken of in religious societies. The church had somehow returned to law—a more brutal and cruel law than had ever been seen in the world to that time.

With the Reformation, Bible-reading Christians came out of every corner of Europe. Tourists went to Israel in those days too, carrying their new King James Bibles and looking for the landmarks in the text. The King James was the "Living Bible" of the day, and though it was frowned upon by those churchmen who thought only the clergy ought to read and interpret the

Now You Don't . . . The Underground Church

Scripture, it became extremely popular. It should be appreciated that people were slain for merely reading this Bible, which some considered obscene and "modern" beyond all spiritual good taste.

But now the light was on.

We don't know a lot about what was happening in the Holy Land. Apparently it was a sleepy land of Turkish farmers, Moslem pilgrims, visiting Christians, and stubbornly steadfast Jews who clung to the soil through it all. But undoubtedly the underground church of Jerusalem was still carrying out its hard ministry, working patiently with whoever happened by the holy sites. Bloody wars came and went as the fertile Promised Land changed hands time and again, but it was as if God had drawn the curtain for awhile so that the land itself might heave a sigh and rest.

Then came World War I and fresh conquerors from all over. When the smoke had cleared, the British were more or less in charge and the Jews were slipping in and establishing the *kibbutzim*. And then came another world war, with its unspeakable Holocaust and the granting of Israel back to the Jews, its rightful owners. The new immigrants inherited the Arab population, the once finely cultivated land they had had to leave to squatters, and the underground church of Jerusalem, still at its post.

In 1967 the Jews, attacked on three fronts, not only defended their land but threw the invaders out of Jerusalem and reestablished the ancient capital of Israel. Not since the time of Jeremiah 2,600 years previously had the Jews truly held sway over God's city.

Of course the Dome, its adherents, and attendant

problems for Judaism remained. And the Christians remained, with their annoying testimony about Jesus.

And now we see the Jews firmly reestablished in Israel, an advanced, enviable modern state. People who know prophecy quiver now at the proximity of our Lord's promises. Now that the Jews have the land and have Jerusalem, it can all happen. Now that the chosen people are back where God started them out, God can conclude His plan for the world.

The Underground Church Today

We can better appreciate the position of those people who make up the underground church in Israel now that we understand the background. Of course those Christians Mal and I met do not trace their lineage back to Hadrian or the Crusades, but they remain in the same position of those loyal ones as far as testifying for Christ is concerned.

Actually, being "born a Christian"—that is, being reared by Christian parents and taken to a church for salvation when the time is right—is easier on an individual than having no Christian lineage. The average Christian in Israel had to make two difficult decisions. All of them had to decide to come to Christ to begin with, of course, and then they had to decide to go to Israel, or stay there, as the case may be. Coming to Christ is easy; working for Him in such a thankless field is the hard part.

It is a testimony in itself to the vital, living faith in Christ that the church of Israel survived at all—that converts are still made in this hard field and that

Now You Don't . . . The Underground Church

people *still* see the validity of the gospel and its relevance to Israel. Mal and I felt deep respect for the Christians we met in Israel. Each one's individual personality fascinated me.*

There's Elichai, for example, whose unique ministry keeps him hopping in Jerusalem government circles. He is a political scientist, an American who graduated from Harvard and Berkeley. Elichai, whose name means "My God Lives," makes it his business to warn the Israelis about approaching prophecies. He is expert on the Bible and thoroughly educated in global political affairs. At the moment, he is keeping an eye trained on Russia and trying to encourage the government to do the same.

I didn't meet Elichai on this particular trip, but he is acknowledged here because he is one of the most tireless workers for the Lord in the entire underground church. Elichai brings the voice of biblical prophecy into the halls of government. He meets with government officials to plead for biblical understanding. He begs them to consider God's Word. Surprisingly, they do not think he is completely crazy. However, they do not trust him completely either, and they don't really think Ezekiel has the latest word on world affairs. Too bad.

If Israel is caught unaware by the Russian invasion or even by the appearance of the Antichrist, it won't be Elichai's fault. Like Jeremiah, he gives names and places about the coming invasion from the north. ("Thus saith the Lord of hosts; Because ye have not heard my words, behold I will send and take all the

---

*Some names and details will be changed throughout this section for obvious reasons.

families of the north . . . and Nebuchadnezzar the king of Babylon, my servant, and will bring them against this land, and against the inhabitants thereof . . ." (Jer. 25:8ff.).

Elichai seems to have stepped right from the pages of the Old Testament, crying out in the wilderness to those who rarely listen, and hopelessly trying to prove the Scriptures to those who have not learned to take them seriously. Sadly, Elichai may well end like Jeremiah himself, crying out his lamentations while Jerusalem burns. Jeremiah concluded his harrowing ministry with the exhausted admission, "Mine eyes do fail with tears . . ." (Lam. 2:11); Elichai may well come to the same pass.

Then there is my good friend Richard whose apartment is always open to footloose Christians. I stayed with him and his roommate, Steve, a young American Hebrew Christian who played the piano at the King David Hotel. Richard is a guide, licensed in five languages, and one of the truly knowledgeable people about Israel today. He guides Christians or Jews through the land with complete appreciation of their preferences. He has a knack for cutting red tape. Through his genius, Mal and I were allowed into the archaeological diggings by the Western Wall to film our movie "The Temple" on a previous trip. Richard graduated from formal studies in both Judaism and Christianity and is the only man I know who may be called either Rabbi or Reverend, depending on where you stand. His witness, when he can extend it, is overwhelming.

Steve is a master musician and the kind of Christian who hums hymns all day under his breath and sings

Now You Don't . . . The Underground Church

"Praise the Lord" whenever he feels like it. He no longer plays the piano at the King David, but has moved to another city where he has a chance to extend his witness through Christian music with other believers. May his music help sanctify his homeland until the coming of the King.

Steve's guitar was the life of the party for me when Mal and I attended the Sabbath dinner at Richard's apartment. It should be appreciated that these Sabbath dinners, held here and there in the underground church, come down to us right from the New Testament. From what I read in the Epistles I think this kind of worship—fellowship, testimonies, prayer together, the Lord's Supper—is the original kind. These Christians, who have no church (as we think of church), prefer to worship around the dinner table on the Sabbath, and you know, so do I! It was lovely.

Richard scared up Christians to attend in the way one might gather a group of spies—let's say there were no printed invitations to this particular dinner. We ended up as a group of worshipers from almost as many nations as are listed in the second chapter of Acts at Pentecost, but we had Jesus in common. That is what the church is supposed to be, whenever possible. That is what it will be in the kingdom!

Mal and I were distressed by the large number of unmarried Christian women in that group. Of marriageable age, they still can't find partners. And who can wonder? They want Christian men, of course, and they are hard to find. And those who are Jewish would really prefer Jewish Christian men, just for the sake of a common background and view of Israel. (You could dig up a lot of gentile Christian men who never give a thought to Israel, but these women wouldn't want them.)

Mal and I talked at length to two women and I found myself encouraging them to keep company on a social level with unbelieving Israelis. It would be an effective witness, I thought, going from my own experience. I was brought to Christ by a pretty Christian girl (now Mrs. Levitt) who persevered in her witness to me and won me to the Lord. I have good experience, personally, with witnessing across the gender line. Anyway, as I argued with the women, when the chips are down we have to reach people whatever way we can. Their own good testimony would impress Israeli men. Feminine modesty appeals deeply to the Jewish sense of decency and the rightness of things.

The underground church is not so much what we think of as a church group as it is a very loosely knit society of rugged individualists in need. This is both its greatest weakness and its greatest strength.

The true picture of the genuine church is not a body, but a bunch of members. They are so diverse in their views, so different in their approaches to the witness in Israel, so remarkably separate in their ministries that one wonders if they ever really do function as a solid body of believers. We saw common worship, of course, but we began to realize that it was the exception rather than the rule.

This would seem to be a great weakness, and it is. But it can be effective. The evangelists—such as their evangelism goes—each seem to have an appeal to a given group in Israel. Like Paul, they adapt them-

Now You Don't . . . The Underground Church

selves to their constituents, each according to his own gifts. As long as the Lord leads the right witness to the right field, it works.

We found the church of Jerusalem very accepting of people who were saved, and by that I mean they love sinners, apparently a lot more than we do. One of the women who attended the Sabbath dinner was a repentant Jewish-American prostitute, formerly from Los Angeles. She was surely forgiven and accepted here. Arab and Russian Christians are welcome.

When a church has to be comprised of only the truly repentant the result includes a lot of characters you might not choose socially. That's what happened in Jerusalem when Jesus was there, and that's what happens there now.

There is enough of the underground church just strewn around town to take care of a lot of undercover witnessing. One government official I know is a solid Christian, deeply sanctified, and inspiring to talk with. At least one aged orthodox Jew sneaks over to the Garden Tomb, the empty tomb of our Lord, and prays before dawn in his full robes.

A girl came from Tel Aviv, Richard recollected, to place a paper prayer in the Wall. This procedure is recommended for those who wish to have God's immediate attention; the prayer is written on a piece of paper and pushed into a crack in the stone in the Western Wall. It is thought that God lives right behind the Wall and will read the prayer immediately. This particular prayer asked if Jesus was the Messiah. A Christian on the scene at the Wall was able to bring that young woman to Christ.

Gordon Walker, a great defender of Israel and a

former resident, shared with me stories of other hearty believers who work the land for Christ, each in his own peculiar way. Together with those already mentioned, they constitute a perfect example of the diversity and yet the oneness of purpose to be found in this unique Holy Land.

There is a kind of true believer who witnesses in Israel and yet finds real acceptance among the population at large. More than one Christian has served the nation in war—normally in a backlines role—and the Israelis do not forget the favor. Vital missions have been accomplished by Christians and they have been decorated for valor. They invariably receive due credit.

An officer of an American Mission who has lived in Israel for several years is such a case. He lost a leg in the attempted rescue of a kidnaped Arab youngster; he followed the kidnaper's trail through a mine field near Jordan. He is a scholar of skill, which the Israeli intellectuals appreciate, and a deeply respected contributor to the linguistic field, an important endeavor in this ancient polyglot land. Held in esteem by university faculty and the public alike, he is honored by both Christians and Jews as a man of faith. He witnesses in a low-key way, but his witness is potent. He knows the rules of the game and he knows his adversaries. He speaks out for the Messiah, but his devotion to the land has more or less earned him the special privilege of expressing this faith.

For a true Christian to earn the regard of the Israelis to the point where they tolerate the witness is an achievement, to say the least. But there is a level of living by faith—in a true walk with God—that im-

Now You Don't . . . The Underground Church

presses all men. Combine it with a real love of the land and you have what the Israelis respect as a welcome guest.

Another witnessing Christian specializes in bringing American Christian youngsters to the Holy Land. This man has achieved official permanent residency in Israel, not an easy thing to accomplish, and operates a *kibbutz* in Judea. The young people he sponsors come not to witness in the streets, of course, but to work. They give service to Israel as volunteer laborers, trading their strength and skills for a daily life in the Promised Land. Instructed by their mentor, they are able workers and sensitive testifiers. They let their labors and their attitudes speak for themselves rather than broadcasting their beliefs at large. "A service of Christian love" is their ideal. They normally help out on the *kibbutzim* and they slowly—oh, so slowly—earn the right to speak from their hearts. The lives they lead and their love testifies more directly than what they are able to say.

The "Garden Tomb Preacher," Rev. Jan Willem van der Hoeven, is well known to Christian tourists who visit the empty final resting place of the Lord. His enthusiastic and inspirational messages, charismatic in tone and soundly biblical, invariably attract a wide variety of pilgrims and more than a few local Israelis. That empty tomb, which caused such consternation in gospel times, still raises the curiosity of the citizens of Jerusalem and is considered by some to be an especially holy shrine.

The ministry of Rev. van der Hoeven extends to the hosting of Dutch visitors and workers, and of course to those of every nation who alight from the endless rows of buses that visit that site. Like the testimony of those who received the Holy Spirit at Pentecost, van der Hoeven's lessons travel widely; they are taken almost everywhere in the world in the hearts of the visitors to the Promised Land.

There are some specialized ministries of witness and counsel to Israelis who have found, or are seeking, the Lord. Among women workers is one who was saved in a foreign nation, though she was an Israeli native, and who counsels with women army personnel. In Israel the women serve in the military and they probably suffer a certain disorientation in their lives as a result. They normally serve in their prime marriageable years, and though they make good soldiers—or more properly, soldiers' assistants—their minds and hearts are often elsewhere. Private Bible study and counsel is available to them through the unique ministry of this one who returned to the land, bringing the Messiah along.

The Roman Catholic charismatic churches are of significance in the ministry of relating to the Israelis. "The Jews require a sign," the Scriptures point out. Healings, tongues, and other signs appeal to a sector of the Jews who appreciate seeing religion in action. There is no question that miracles impress Jewish people, as they do anyone else. If "tongues are for a sign" (1 Cor. 14:22), then the Jews have sign-posts available all over Israel.

The ministries of people like Mal and others who work with Israeli officials on projects like films and news reports from the land must also be included among the efforts of the true church, though they're not really underground. The pastors who lead tours, the foreign Christians who come on business, and the born-again visitors who range from mere diggers in the archaeological sites to eminent scholars of history and its relics all bring a witness. Tracts are passed around, cautious street witnessing is undertaken—probably more among the Arabs than the Jews—and fellowship continues to grow between guests and hosts in Israel. Understandably, more direct witnessing is tolerated from visitors on official business than from local Christians. The government certainly does not censure the testimonies of those who come to the land on projects beneficial to the land, and it does not keep a watch on visitors as the Iron Curtain countries do.

And so the lonely, difficult work goes on in the Holy Land. The true church works almost without fellowship or commendation. It is highly fragmented, having altogether little identity as a unified body. It is alive but suffering, and of course greatly in need of help. Prayer and people are needed.

7.
Some Like It Cold...
The Quasi-Church

"I know thy works," said Jesus of the Laodiceans, whose church showed certain faults, "that thou art neither cold nor hot" (Rev. 3:15). Apparently one couldn't convict that church of having lost its faith entirely, but one wouldn't expect a big blessing there either.

They were lukewarm and the Lord abhorred that: "So then because thou art lukewarm, and neither cold nor hot, I will spue thee out of my mouth" (Rev. 3:16).

We can all appreciate the image. We like our coffee hot and our milk cold, but did you ever sip from a tepid water fountain on a summer day?

Well, we found that the church in Israel varies from boiling to freezing, conservative to liberal, orthodox to apostate—however you like to think of it. In this land where eighty languages are spoken among three million people, you can *really* go to the church of your choice. And undoubtedly, some like it cold.

The Underground Church of Jerusalem

The Law-keeping Church

A Bible study that Mal and I attended in Tel Aviv gave us a taste of a kind of teaching going on under the Christian label. Getting to and from that Bible study was half the battle. Tel Aviv is a Westernized madhouse of traffic and hustle-bustle with everyone seeming as if they are in a perpetual hurry.

We drove out over the main expressway from Jerusalem, watching the sides of the road for the rust-proofed military vehicles left there from the 1948 War of Independence. Those Arab troop carriers, jeeps, and even tanks were left in their places, wherever they were stopped, and painted with a brown rustproofer. They stand there at the roadside like so many foreboding ghosts, constantly reminding the people of Israel what it took to get this land back.

We were almost late for the study because Mal enjoys showing off his intimate knowledge of the Holy Land; he refused to ask for directions through the maze of Tel Aviv. We drove through some woods on the edge of the city, following one of Mal's "shortcuts," but ended up looking down a sentry's rifle. Mal had driven us to a hidden army camp. We did a lot of smiling and chattering in Hebrew and English and they let us make a U-turn.

It was a harrowing experience after days of clearing those highway checkpoints around Jerusalem. There the soldiers set up roadblocks and look into each car, especially watching the Arabs, of course, but giving foreigners a close going over as well. So we were experienced at looking harmless by this time. (Of course we *were* harmless, but the Israeli troops like

Some Like It Cold . . . The Quasi-Church

people who are *very* harmless.) The most effective pose was for me to be silent and to act somewhat annoyed, as though I were the boss of this particular excursion; we hoped my Israeli face would reassure the soldiers. Our rented-car license plate helped matters; Palestinian guerrillas rarely rent their vehicles from Hertz of Israel.

The Bible study was underway when we arrived at the apartment in central Tel Aviv. An interesting cast of characters was present. They seemed to be largely Gentiles, but I was fascinated to see a huge and menacing Israeli athlete, undoubtedly a soccer player, intently following the lesson in his Bible. People think of Israelis as wiry little characters who accomplish their purposes through cunning rather than strength, but this fellow could have been an Oakland Raider lineman. His muscles bulged out of his team shirt and his shorts, and the Bible in his huge paws looked like it was pocket-size, although it was a big hardback.

And it was no wonder he concentrated with all he had on this particular lesson. It was on Jewish law and very complex. It was unlike the sort of Bible study we experience in the States in that it dealt with extremely minute details of tribal rulings of Deuteronomy—how many generations must pass before the descendants of a convert to Judaism may become lawful members of a given tribe, and so forth. "Samson" squinted at the complexities.

This struck me, as I listened, as going too far the other way. I am always telling Christians to get their noses out of the Epistles once in a while and open the Old Testament for some real background and principle. But the intensive study of the old laws, without

The Underground Church of Jerusalem

mention of the Messiah or His covenant, seemed somehow too oblique for me. I could barely follow the intricacies of the study, even with an open Bible.

The teacher was articulate and interesting and seemingly possessed an endless knowledge of the law, citing passages from the *Talmud*, the *Mishna*, the *Zohar*, and the other Jewish commentaries on the Scriptures. My own knowledge of these matters is limited; I didn't think any Christian concerned himself with such orthodox data anymore.

But in talking with the teacher afterwards I met a new kind of Christian.

He believed in the Messiah, but he believed in the law too. He covered all bases. That man was *really* saved, you might say. He was prepared to meet God on any of His terms; whatever covenant God preferred, this disciple could qualify.

Now that's not correct doctrine as we look at things from a biblical perspective. After all, if the Messiah came to free us from the law, what business have we putting ourselves under the law again? Shall we sew up the torn veil in the Holy Place? Shall we rebuild that wall of partition which once separated those under the law from those who had no law? Shall we repeat the error of the Galatian church to whom Paul had to write, "Are ye so foolish? Having begun in the Spirit are ye now made perfect by the flesh?" (Gal. 3:3).

Shall we reject liberty in Christ?

I brought up these questions to the teacher in our talk afterward, and he sighed as if to say, "Here comes the Americans again, folks. Let's make things crystal clear for them." He explained to me that Jews are responsible to keep the law and that's all there is to it. God's will doesn't change. Gentiles don't have to keep the law, but Jews do. Even if they have the Messiah, Jews must keep the law because God required it of them originally.

"Boy, does that ever take the fun out of salvation," I told him. "I thought Jesus paid up my sins on the cross."

"Yes, He did," the teacher allowed, "but you are a Jew and if you want to call yourself a Jew you must behave like a Jew. Don't you call yourself a 'Jewish Christian'?" he asked me.

"I certainly do," I told him.

"Well, then, act like a Jew. The trouble with the Jews is they want to be Jews without doing what is necessary to be Jewish."

Somehow I liked that guy. He was smart. He spoke perfect Hebrew, Yiddish, English, and the language of the European country from which he had emigrated to Israel, and he was obviously steeped in Scripture.

But I couldn't agree with him. The sort of law he quoted from the commentaries was out of the Oral Tradition, which says that Moses came down from the Mount with much more law than we have preserved in the Scriptures. The rest he *told* to the people, and they repeated it down through the millennia. It was copied down in writing after the temple destruction by Rabbi Akiba and others, lest it be lost among a dispersed nation, but it was dependable and it was God's will.

I have trouble believing it because I know some of it departs from Scripture to a dangerous degree. (The separation of the dishes is a harmless, but pointed, example.) I also fear that this law-keeping Christianity may become like some of the coldest churches by holding the works of sages to be more authoritative than the Bible.

The oral law seemed to change with the Jewish climate through the centuries. So nowadays sacrifices are said to be unnecessary for Jewish fellowship with God—good deeds (*mitzvah*) will do it. This convenient revision of one of God's most basic admonitions came into being after the temple destruction in A.D. 70 and it satisfied the cry of a dispersed people—"My God, what will happen to us now that we can't sacrifice?"

That's bad business. Take out the sacrifices and you take out the enormity of sin. Take out the sacrifices and you take out the meaning of the Messiah's first coming (Isa. 53). The vast majority of Jews today don't think they *need* to be saved, and these are the descendants of those who offered sacrifices to Jehovah for 2,000 years!

And worst of all, get rid of the sacrifice concept and there is no reason for the Crucifixion in the Jewish mind. The average Jew has little to say on why Jesus, an essentially good man, was executed. Too revolutionary, too disturbing, too humane for His time; that's the best they can estimate about the sacrifice that gave true salvation to the world.

So I am not about to look into the Jewish peripheral laws, nor to try to keep them.

But my opponent in this debate made an interesting point. He went on, "Look now, all people make new laws, and that's just the nature of men. They have to have something to *obey*. I just feel that the Oral Tradition, taken from the Scriptures as it was and written down by faithful Jews, has more validity than the church laws that come along through the years. Look at you American Christians. You are worried about drinking and smoking and gambling and dancing. That stuff has nothing to do with the Scriptures either, but in some of your churches you act as though those prohibitions are the heart of Christianity."

He had me there.

He and I would perfectly agree on what the New Testament says by way of Christian behavior, of course. The point was, he obeyed all of that and he obeyed all of his Oral Tradition on top of it. And to give some idea of how *much* law there is to obey in the Oral Tradition, there are 416 sections, with 8 to 20 divisions per section, in the *Talmud* concerning *the Sabbath alone*—thousands of individual laws about how to rest on Saturdays!

On a previous trip I experienced the weight of the Sabbath law in Israel on those who keep it. I was in an orthodox hotel and my room was on the twelfth floor. I took the elevator down on a Saturday morning and I noticed that it stopped at every floor even though no one was waiting. I went to the desk clerk and told him the elevator was on the blink, but he said, "No it's not. We pre-set it that way for you so you wouldn't have to push the button on the Sabbath"!

The Sabbath laws prescribe how many yards one may walk on the Sabbath, what light chores one may or may not do, and endless little prohibitions and allowances. One inconvenient law concerns operating a light switch; it may *not* be done on the Sabbath. Therefore, orthodox synagogues may not legally switch on the lights on Saturday morning for the worship. They get around this one—those who take it seriously—by appointing a neighborhood Gentile to come in and do this for them, and to turn them off at the end of the service. My dear friend Dr. Thomas S. McCall, a Jewish evangelist of consummate skill and dedication, once served as the *Shabbas Goy* (Yiddish for "Sabbath Gentile") in a storefront synagogue in Los Angeles. He was thus privileged to hang around for the worship (but not to participate in it). He was actually able to witness for Christ, after a fashion, as he came to be trusted by the congregation.

But the teacher might have made a very good point. All men make laws—new laws all the time—so that they can obey something difficult. And they often make things more difficult for themselves than God ever intended. The very idea of God being a taskmaster who keeps a score on how well we obey laws is not Christian, but Christians fall into this all the time. When we're hot enough, we want to be hotter.

The law-keeping Jewish church is unlike the visible church and unlike the underground church. It is part of a third entity we might call "The Quasi-Church." It has a strange doctrine, but it *is* part of the true church; its adherents believe in Jesus Christ and salvation through *Him*. They keep the law because they want to but they wouldn't dream of salvation outside of the Messiah's sacrifice.

The God Who Has No Sons

Under the heading of quasi-churches we run into every sort of permutation of Christianity imaginable.

Some Like It Cold . . . The Quasi-Church

The strangest case of quasi-church belief concerns groups who believe in Jesus but who don't believe He was God's son. They say, "Jesus was the Messiah and He is our Savior. We believe in the Cross and we believe in the Resurrection. *But* He was not God's Son because God has no sons. God is One."

True enough, the Old Testament assures us, if it doesn't say anything else, that God is one. This is what set the Jews apart from the pagans—monotheism. The Jews pray, perfectly scripturally, "Hear, O Israel, the Lord our God, *the Lord is One.*"

Now it's argued that the Lord is one *unity*, since the Hebrew word used for "One," *echad*, may accurately mean "unity." It is also argued that this very prayer contains a hidden key to the trinity—God's name is said three times. But however one objects, the Jews read "One," and some of them take that very seriously.

If Jesus wasn't God's Son, who do they say He was? (He asked the same question, didn't He? "Whom do men say that I . . . am?") Well, they say He was God's prime Anointed One (translation: Messiah) with the mission of providing salvation to the world. Their doctrine is exactly like that of any Bible church over here, but they don't like the Father-Son relationship. They are saved by grace, but they stick on this point.

I argued the issue by saying that Scripture itself says Jesus was God's Son. Didn't *He* say that? Didn't *God* say, "This is my beloved Son, in whom I am well pleased"? Didn't Jesus say a hundred times, "*My* Father," as opposed to "*Our* Father"? "Yes, yes," they would answer, "but you must understand. The Bible was written for simple folk, even Gentiles, and they understand these things best when some kind of image or analogy is used. The Father-Son relationship only describes the God-and-Anointed-One closeness of relationship so that people could appreciate that Jesus really did come with God's special assignment. If He had said He was a high priest or a prophet, then He would have been the same as a long line of past Jewish leaders. He had to be somebody special in our way of thinking, and so God describes Him as His Son. That's all."

The virgin birth, then, becomes highly suspect, as is Mary's conception. But then they might argue, "Mary wasn't really Jesus' most dependable follower anyway. You can see that *she* didn't understand her oldest boy as being God's Son at all."

What bothers me here is that there are many anointed ones in the Scriptures. Even King Cyrus of Persia was God's anointed one (Isa. 45:1) because he released the captive Israelites to rebuild the temple in the sixth century B.C. Jesus loses His very special standing when the Sonship is denied. Personally, I like the Scriptures exactly as written. God is one, yes, but He is expressed in three Persons. Further, He appeared to Abraham as a flame, His Spirit moved over the waters at the beginning of creation. And it is within the powers of the Maker of the universe and mankind to send His Son to the earth.

We should appreciate, coming as we do out of a church-oriented society of Christianity over here, that traditional behavior in the Middle East varies quite a bit from what we conceive of as a proper Christian walk. The "11-A.M.-Sunday-in-English" syndrome is the first piece of American Christian behavior that does not go over very well in Israel. The first missionaries to Israel held their services in English, "the biblical language," at 11:00 A.M. on Sunday mornings, knowing that God expected to hear from them at exactly that time. The Israelis certainly ignored those goings-on. The Western culture didn't fit in with the Israeli Sabbath and it didn't fit in with the religious customs of people used to worshiping God every day at all hours. English is not God's language in Israel, needless to say, but the missionaries traditionally could not read the Bible in Hebrew.

Similarly, Jehovah, according to orthodox Israeli reckoning, does not have sons. Some Israelis come to Jesus for salvation, they believe in Him and trust Him and know that He was resurrected, and they believe that He is coming back to restore His kingdom; but they do not believe He was God's literal Son, coequal with the Father.

You figure it out.

The Plural Covenant

Another serious departure from biblical doctrine is the "plural covenant," which attempts to say that the Jews are already saved and do not need Jesus. Those who hold to this idea believe Jesus came for the rest of the world—the Gentiles. The Jews will make it into heaven under the Law, assuming they are keeping it. Even if they are not keeping it, the God who chose them will not forsake them. He knows their faults, but has always stood by them anyway.

We are wasting our time trying to witness to them, according to this reasoning, since they are already taken care of. The reason they don't come to Christ in any great numbers, these people believe, is because the Holy Spirit is not working on them. Some do come, with special missions, like Paul and a remnant through the centuries, but the others are already saved. The plural covenant holds that there are two covenants in force now, one for the Jews and one for the Gentiles.

This gets into some complex scriptural arguments but seems to fall devastatingly on the fact of Jesus' coming "only unto the lost sheep of the house of Israel." The plural covenant folks say that He really came to *disciple* the Jews and that He succeeded in that—they went out and brought in the Gentiles. He used the already-saved Jews to reach the lost Gentiles.

A plural covenant believer, and Israel is filled with them, is hard to witness to. If you present Christ he says, "Fine, certainly I believe He was the Messiah. Thank God you are saved by Him. I'll be glad to see you in the kingdom to come. But I am already with God through my forefathers and our own covenant. Thanks just the same."

This particular angle on the Bible allows the Jews to honor gentile salvation through Christ without becoming involved themselves. It spares them the problem of wondering why salvation seems to work so well through Christ—it was supposed to, *for Gentiles*. As for the Jews, they were all certified long ago and we can quit worrying about them.

I have the feeling there is a whiff of satanic anti-Semitism about this whole thing. By providing such easy exemption from the gospel for the Jews, these zealots disenfranchise themselves and others from their own Messiah. Jews would never be saved under the plural covenant, at least not as we understand salvation by Christ and His sacrifice.

People believing the plural covenant cannot be listed as part of the church since they do not really believe in Jesus for salvation (at least not for the Jews). They are "on the line" because they *do* think He was the Messiah and that He provides salvation, but only for the Gentiles. This denies major scriptural precepts, but the plural covenant is one step closer to the church than the more usual Jewish position which holds that salvation by Christ is purely a Gentile invention and that only the Jews have been chosen. But the next step is the biggie—true salvation for Jews through Christ. They don't take that step, thinking they are already saved.

"False" Baptisms

There is another kind of quasi-Christian found in Israel—those who were baptized as children in Europe during World War II. I met a guide named *Chaim* (Life) whose parents had him baptized soon after the Nazi takeover so that he could be a Christian and not have the liability of being a Jew. And some of those baptisms influenced the people later in life. Chaim calls himself a Christian today, some thirty-five years later. He knows no New Testament, does not worship Christ or attend a church of any kind, and does not really understand salvation as the true historic church regards it. But he respects Jesus and calls himself a "follower." "My life has been a real *Via Dolorosa*," Chaim told me, more or less summing up the position of those with no assurance of salvation. It is a testimony to the horror of the anti-Semitism in Europe that some Jews resorted to false baptisms to escape certain death. This part of the quasi-church is really nonfunctional as a church, but I understand that some of the baptized ones tend to look to Christ in prayer, feeling that they are distant members of His covenant.

We must at least appreciate the power of those childhood baptisms. They inspire some of the "converts" even after decades. How does God look upon those lonely and forgotten ones, primarily orphans, who came at least into the water to seek deliverance? It is sad that there are so few to lift them up.

The Formalistic Church

The last category of the quasi-church in Israel is the large number of liberal and "form-of-godliness" churches of all stripes which dot the Holy Land. Each one would have to be studied as to its sincerity and purpose to see if there is work of any value being done toward the kingdom of Christ, but they certainly proliferate in Israel and they are the average Israeli's idea of what the Christian church is all about.

"The Israel Economist" puts out a pamphlet, which I picked up at a government information office in Jerusalem, entitled "The Christian Churches in the State of Israel: A Survey by Dr. S. P. Colbi" Dr. Colbi was an attorney who served the Israel Ministry of Religious Affairs as an expert in Canon Law until his retirement in 1975. He was awarded the Order of Commander of St. Gregory the Great by the Holy See.

Some Like It Cold . . . The Quasi-Church

Dr. Colbi's twenty-four-page study (available at Box 7052, Jerusalem) deals exclusively with what we would call liberal or formalistic churches. He divides the churches of Israel into four categories: Catholic, Orthodox, Monophysite, and Protestant. Evangelical churches would fall into the last category, more than likely, but Dr. Colbi does not mention them. The booklet is strewn with photos of churchmen in gradiose robes shaking the hands of government officials. (One such churchman was jailed for Palestinian gun-running a year ago.)

This sad account barely mentions the Messiah or what the churches are doing to bring His gift of salvation to Israel. The churches are given credit for the humane institutions they have founded and continue to operate, and there are impressive pictures of ceremonies of much pomp with the prelates in their parade dress. But you would not look into this study for the progress of the true church.

Naturally the government office does not hand out booklets about the witnessing efforts in the Holy Land or how many people have been saved. But the sad part is that this booklet gives a true picture of what many Israelis think the church is: a bunch of bearded old patriarchs all dressed in garish costumes, carrying holy things in their hands and smiling at the camera in public postures of friendliness.

It is no wonder that the Israeli is not too impressed. Nobody would be. We have allowed the testimony of the Galilean, who had only one robe and no place to lay his head, to rest almost entirely in the hands of grandly costumed play-church politicians.

8.
"Never Again!"

Some gentile Christians are perplexed as to just *why* the Jewish people reject the gospel so completely. It would seem that evangelizing Israel would be just the same as evangelizing any other nation—even easier, considering the heritage, the Bible, and the very sites of the Lord's own ministry in the land.

But the most stalwart of missionaries turn pale at the very idea of taking the gospel back home to the Holy Land. Jewish resistance to God's best plans, which began in the wilderness when the infuriated Moses broke God's tablets at the sight of the golden calf, goes on. Churches omit the land of the Lord in their missionary support. It is taken for granted that these people are too hard to save and that's all there is to that. Jews are too resistant.

I'm sure glad there were some Christians who didn't think that way when *my* turn came!

In this chapter I want to look carefully at the nature of the Israeli resistance to the gospel. It takes peculiar and very interesting forms, but it is hardly insurmountable.

The Underground Church of Jerusalem

Fear of Genocide

Deep in the Israeli psyche is *fear*. Fear has been a part of Jewish culture from the beginning and we need not wonder why. It is not unreasonable for Jews to fear the world; the world has massacred the Jewish race tirelessly through the entire length of recorded history. The Jew has never lived without fear.

Now the average Israeli doesn't look afraid as he walks down the street. Quite the contrary, in fact. There is a bravado about Israelis that can be felt everywhere in the land and it deeply impresses visitors. These people look as if they could take on the whole world, and maybe they can.

But in little corners of the culture, in little things seen by the one who observes Israel, the old fear is evident still.

Fear of Christians, thoroughly justified through past experience with those cross-carrying butchers of the Middle Ages (and even in this century in Eastern Europe and Russia), is manifest in little things. That abhorrence of the cross—demonstrated by such practices as the use of the "T" instead of the plus sign in arithmetic—is practically inbred in Israel. The myriad rules and regulations about witnessing, the inattention to prophecy, and the purposeful ignoring of the presence of evangelical Christianity in the land all add up to a very real fear of the New Covenant and its Author. Jesus is not an Israeli citizen anymore; His visa was canceled long ago.

King Herod was the first to develop a deep-felt fear of Jesus, perhaps because he believed prophecy implicitly. He had been warned that a new king was to

"Never Again!"

come out of Bethlehem, and so he went to the extraordinary trouble of building a mountain palace to overlook that small town day and night (and also to be able to survey the Judean valley out to the Dead Sea for signs of an attack from that sector). There are no substantial mountains in Judea, and so Herod was obliged to have one made. On and on, for what must have been several years, soil was piled up until Herod had his mountain from which he could watch Bethlehem and its environs and even Jerusalem in the distance. It just shows what can be done with public funds and 50,000 slaves.

Herod did all that just to keep an eye on the birthplace of the coming Messiah! The gospel recounts the tragic story of the murdering of the male babies of Bethlehem while the infant Jesus with His parents escaped to Egypt. God had said through the prophet: "I . . . called my son out of Egypt" (Hos. 11:1), and so He did.

Herod tried to cover all possibilities, but as the Lord said, "It is written." Jesus, the King of the Jews, was born, according to the written prophecies: "Unto us a child is born, a son is given . . . (Isa. 9:6); "But thou Bethlehem . . ." (Mic. 5:2); "A virgin shall conceive . . ." (Isa. 7:14). He survived in spite of the fanatic fear of King Herod. Jesus survived the ravaging of Bethlehem and He went on to confront Israel with the kingdom of God, running into the first organized Jewish resistance to the gospel. Most of the Jews of Israel are no more open to the gospel now than their forefathers were then.

Fear is just a fact of the daily experience in Israel. Mal and I visited the campus of Hebrew University,

The Underground Church of Jerusalem

which is situated high on Mount Scopus. It overlooks much of Jerusalem on the one side and the vast wilderness of Judea on the other. There we saw what was clearly a modern institution of higher learning combined with what is undoubtedly a military fortress. The walls of the university building are made of thick stone; radar towers with much antennae and machinery dominate the skyline. The underground parking areas have wide accesses and high clearances; tanks and big guns could operate from that advantageous position against the same attack from the Dead Sea sector feared by Herod. The area looked more like a series of underground bunkers than a college campus; mysterious holes in the walls, commanding ground-level perspective, were everywhere. We called the place "Fortress Jerusalem."

You can't blame them for being ready, under the circumstances. But that very reasonable fear of the outside world in terms of military attack spills over into a fear of the outside world even in terms of religion. The Israelis want nothing from anybody, I perceived, except to be allowed to live in peace. They would prefer to be alone in this world than to have to defend their land and their lifestyle at every turn. *No outsiders are rejoiced over*, and particularly not those who could change the Israeli way of doing things. Evangelists may therefore be accorded the same wariness as enemy troops.

Consider again the orthodox Jews and their laws. Their religion is a lifestyle. It is a complete way of living. Once you enter the *Mea Shearim* you have stepped back into a world that existed in its prime nineteen centuries ago. It is, in the Israeli view, suffi-

"Never Again!"

ciently sanctified and sufficiently related to God's will and needs to brook no intrusion from outsiders.

Mal and I passed a huge banner stretched across a major street in the *Mea Shearim* that read, "YOUNG GIRLS, THE *TORAH* SAYS YOU MUST DRESS MODESTLY." Mal and I couldn't think where the *Torah* says that, though we knew well the New Testament does. But if a sign across your street says that the matter is already adequately covered, you don't need a new holy book.

Of course, we could see the chinks in the orthodox armor. The confectionary stores of the *Mea Shearim* have the whiskey bottles lined up on the back shelves. Johnny Walker Scotch, in all its Westernized sophistication, was available by the quart for the private problems of the proudly costumed priests of the *Talmud*. We longed to tell somebody that true faith is totally sufficient; the one who follows the Messiah needs no equalizer to combat this life.

We did, of course, witness to that precious eighty-year-old American flower seller right on the street, and I will remember his dialogue as long as I live. He told us that he had come to Israel five years before on a tour, looked the place over, and when the tour pulled out simply told his fellow travelers, "I'm staying!" He gave us a hearing, probably because we were Americans, and he remains in our prayers. A man who would give up everything at the age of seventy-five to sell flowers in a Jerusalem street must be especially loved of God. We hope to see him in God's house. It will be a great day in heaven if he's there to say, "I believed what you told me."

The orthodox guard their lifestyles very jealously,

and who can blame them? Everybody from Pharoah to Hitler has tried to take it away from them, and people are still trying. That's presumably why some orthodox Jews who actually believe in Jesus still keep the law.

Jews are like that. They were forced to wear the Star of David on their coats and they wear it still, but now with pride.

Christians are like that too. The world tried to get rid of Jesus on a cross and now you find that cross around the necks of Christians and atop their churches. Godly people hang onto the very symbols by which they were supposed to be defeated, and the orthodox Jews are surely no exception.

The degree to which keeping the law is a true lifestyle can best be demonstrated by the moss-covered fence we saw near Ben Gurion Airport. We were curious about it; a lot of work had gone into sowing a high wooden barrier along the expressway with thick moss, which made it opaque. A taped program by American Jewish actor Herschel Bernardi explained it on the El Al plane we took home; the moss shields the eyes of the people of a little hamlet back in the trees from even *seeing* people driving cars on the Sabbath!

It may all come back to fear—fear of being made non-Jewish. That was God's prime penalty for law-breaking in the *Torah*: "You shall be cut off from among your people!"

Personally, speaking as a Jew, I would have a terrible fear of losing my Jewishness if that were possible. And it *was* possible under the Old Covenant. Obviously if one was cut off from among the only people who were chosen, then one had no further chance to come to God. It was tantamount to losing one's salvation.

"Never Again!"

Unregenerate Jews often accuse me of having thrown away my own Jewishness by my belief in the Messiah, but actually that was the way I found it. Jesus *is* Jewish.

But the fear of being changed pervades the mind of the Israeli. He has waited so long, fought so hard, and weathered so many storms that now he simply wants to claim his land and his traditions in peace. He wants to be what his ancestors were. He does not want Jesus because his ancestors did not generally believe in Jesus.

Naturally the Holocaust of World War II has great bearing on the Jewish fear of the rest of the world. Didn't the world stand aside, blissfully unaware or uncaring of the genocide going on in Hitler's camps? Didn't even the Christian churches of Germany manage to look the other way in every village when the Nazis packed their Jewish neighbors into those cattle trains? Did anyone anywhere show any concern at all that God's chosen people were being slaughtered by the millions?

I toured the *Yad wa-Shem* (Holocaust) alone. It's a memorial to the six million lost. I purposely took that depressing tour on a day when Mal was busy elsewhere. I wanted, for one thing, to pay respect to my own missing family members.

It's a beautiful memorial park set high on Mount Herzl to the southwest of Jerusalem. One enters through a promenade of lovely plants and small trees, which flourish despite the rocky soil. I began seeing name plates among the flowers and on pedestals between the trees—gentile names. I came to an explanatory maker which specified that a tree or a plant had been placed in the park in memory of every

The Underground Church of Jerusalem

gentile family who had helped the Jewish people during the Nazi terror.

There were many Corrie ten Booms, thank God, throughout the countries of Europe who helped the Jews hide from the Nazis or escape from the danger areas. Israel has painstakingly tracked down the names of every family reportedly giving help, however minimal, and they will be remembered in this singular setting forever. As to how many were genuine Christians, nobody cares. These were the humane people, the guardians of what was right. In many cases they had grievously endangered themselves to help the Jews, and the Jews have not forgotten.

I walked slowly through the exhibits in this terrifying museum, where items of the dead and vivid evidence of the murders were on display. There was a striped prison uniform, copies of the bids made by German companies volunteering to supply the ovens used to bake the millions of corpses into ashes, and photographs of the mass graves. There was the picture, now famous among Jews everywhere, of the little boy, maybe six years old, standing by the barrier to the Warsaw Ghetto and holding out his pathetically empty hands to a Nazi officer. Was that haunting face saying, "See, I've stolen no food"? Or, "Take me, sir, but leave my family alone"? Or were those extended hands, palms up, simply making the ultimate gesture of resignation: "Here I am. Kill me."

There was a carefully recorded story of the heroes of the Warsaw Ghetto who defended their sewers and holes in the walls against German regulars for so long that the Nazis had to burn them out, building by

"Never Again!"

building, as if they were rats. The Germans, thinking they had starved and burned the Jews into submission, found it necessary to call up seige guns to defeat the unarmed skeletons that remained to defend the ghetto.

If they fought that way to hold a miserable few blocks of ghetto, how shall they act when Israel is attacked?

The final room of the exhibit caught me totally by surprise, as it was designed to do. It was a very dark room and it took a moment for my eyes to pick out what I was looking at. There were odd shapes all around me, and as my eyes became adjusted to the darkness I saw that I was standing among tombstones.

There was a tombstone for each European country in which Jews were killed. A number was etched in gold on the black surface of each stone. No further explanation was needed. The numbers ran into the millions for some of those countries.

Please believe me when I tell you that tears came to my eyes when I walked among those tombstones.

I didn't know which stones counted up my own family in that awful room, but some of my family are included in those numbers. In any case, it didn't matter. I wasn't crying for my immediate family, but for the family of Israel and the family of mankind.

And I can tell you that if I were a non-Christian Israeli, I would be saying, just as they say, "Leave me alone; I'll make it with what I have."

The Holocaust completely explains the Jewish fears of almost anything outside the Jewish community. I dare say *any* people who had gone through this would be very afraid of a great many things even thirty years later. Israeli resistance to the rest of the world, Christianity included, rests solidly on this brutal massacre which stands alone in all the world's history of man's inhumanity.

The slogan of the tough Jewish Defense League (JDL), arch-enemy of Christian evangelism among Jews everywhere, is "Never Again." The world will never again hear, "I'm Jewish. Kill me."

It's interesting, and germane to my point here, that the JDL fights so hard against evangelism among Jews when their slogan actually concerns the Holocaust. It shows how the two run together—both the Holocaust and the idea of Jews becoming Christians amount to genocide in their minds. If Jews become Christians, they feel, then the Jews are Jews no more. Firebombings of Jewish-Christian missions and the beating of a missionary to the Jews in New York City have ensued from the efforts of these peacemakers, according to reports from the American Board of Missions to the Jews.

Aversion to Non-Jewish Culture

Of course Israeli resistance to the gospel is not all based on fear. Christianity simply isn't Jewish in the Israeli mind; in fact it is a lot less Jewish than it ought to be, or once was. And Israelis like things Jewish, just as Americans like things American.

Israel has its own peculiar culture and it is not in the market for anything new. It's just a young country, but it has its own way of doing things already. Christianity comes as an intruder, at least in the way it is usually presented by Christians.

"Never Again!"

The average Israeli young woman wouldn't care for Campus Crusade for Christ or an American-style Baptist church partly because of their dress codes. The well-dressed Israeli lady wears a black turtleneck, fancy high heels, lots of jewelry, and Levis. (People everywhere fail to appreciate that Levis are Jewish-made blue jeans, named for my very own tribe!) The Levis are worn long for the day's work and cuffed to the knee over hose for the evening's outing.

I saw Gerber Baby Food in the Super Sol, a Jerusalem supermarket where I went to buy the chickens for Richard's Sabbath dinner, but the baby on the label was Israeli. They like it *their* way.

Much of Western culture doesn't appeal to Israelis. They don't like violence and we have plenty. In Jerusalem any woman can walk along the streets in perfect safety at midnight.

And they already have a mission. Some Christians try to appeal to the Israelis, when they get a chance, by telling them about the Christian vision and the life of service. But the Israelis all have a mission—to stay alive and keep the country secure—and their lives of service are cut out for them in the land.

As long as the people of Israel are on the defensive against the rest of the world, they will be resistant to the gospel, which they think of as belonging solely to outsiders. As long as there are checkpoints along the roads, as long as gunboats patrol the Tel Aviv beaches at night, and as long as people hate Jews, the evangelism will be very difficult. It would take a whole book just to tell about the infinite security measures in effect throughout this little land. People in such a position do not care about various religious philosophies; they simply want to live safely.

The Underground Church of Jerusalem

There's resistance too from the sophisticated folk of Tel Aviv, a busy modern city rather like Los Angeles or New York. There the life is secular and up-to-date. The Christians who show up are regarded as far too conservative and dull by the local Israelis. Tel Aviv is not "sin city" by any means, but it is an alive and humming place—a young city—and it will require the witness of vibrant young Christians who can confront the Israelis with something better than their own zest for life. Thus far, Christians in Tel Aviv are usually laughed off as a minor nuisance.

And Gentiles just do not rate in Tel Aviv society (in the same manner that Jews don't rate in some American country clubs). Mal, plainly a Gentile, actually drew unfriendly stares from passers-by, I noticed. The punchline came when we were greeted by our chambermaid the night we stayed in the Dan Hotel in Tel Aviv. She greeted me privately, "Welcome home."

It is interesting to notice that Israeli resistance to evangelism and conversion only applies to the Christian kind—other religions are somehow considered "safe" for Jews. Thus Mal and I saw people on the beach at dawn in Tel Aviv doing yoga meditations and exercises. I have already mentioned the presence of Moonies, witches, and the whole collection of the latest cults to be found around the world these days. For some reason it's possible to join such groups and still be Jewish in Israel. I just don't understand how that is, but if you want to be a yogi, you can be a Jewish yogi; but if you want to be a Christian, you *can't* be a Jewish Christian. When you become a Christian your Jewishness somehow goes away from

"Never Again!"

you in the night, but you can be a Jewish Hindu or a Jewish Moonie or even a Jewish Satanist.

Christianity certainly has a bad press over there.

Think how hard it would be to witness to an orthodox Jew doing yoga exercises on an Israeli beach! When do we leave for New Guinea?

It should be appreciated that Israel is largely made up of immigrants and that these immigrants came from "gospel-resistant" Jewish communities to begin with.

Jews come to Israel mainly from Europe, the United States, and Russia, but of course there are Jews all over the world. The problems Jews have faced in Europe, the United States, and Russia are all very different but the resistance to the gospel developed out of much the same things. In all three societies Jews are second-class citizens, a minority group.

In Europe the Holocaust was enough to make Jews abhor the place forevermore, but they had previous troubles which we have already talked about. The lack of love and concern shown by the true church over the years left Jews with the feeling that the gospel was certainly somebody else's. Cruel anti-Semitic church doctrines through the Middle Ages are well remembered by the Jewish emigrants to Israel.

In the United States the Jews enjoy religious freedom, but that same second-class stigma hangs on. The Jews have to be doctors, lawyers, or high-powered businessmen if they are to make it in America. The American church has so little discernible witness to the Jews going on that the vast majority of Jews have never even heard of the concept that a Jew may be a Christian. Much lip service is given to

Jewish witnessing in our churches, and some does go on, but when the Lord asks, "How did you treat my brothers?" there are going to be some embarrassed Americans.

Although Jews were among those who settled this nation originally and greatly helped to build it into a mighty force in two centuries, this is still a "Christian" (gentile) nation. The "Christian principles" we like to speak of this nation being founded upon were originally Jewish principles. But who ever heard of anyone saying, "That's showing a real Jewish spirit." The missionaries of the American Board of Missions to the Jews have always had to contend with the majority of churches who somehow forget to call in for decades on end. My face and my name aren't quite right for speaking in most of America's churches, it's safe to say. It's okay for me to write a book, of course, but then I'm not asking to marry your daughter, am I?

Things are a lot worse in Russia. While the American who emigrates to Israel thinks of the American church as coldly gentile and not open to him, the Russian emigrant thinks of the Russian "Christian" church, such as it is, as a deadly enemy. Russia has been at war against the Jews for quite some time now.

In Russia the Jews are still persecuted, and only international pressures inspired by Jewish organizations can seem to get them out. I have two Russian Jewish friends now who were recently spirited out from behind the Iron Curtain; both are saved. They were brought up as atheists, it being too difficult to maintain Judaism in Russia, and they were beaten by "Christians" on Good Friday as youths.

Some Russian Jews get altogether turned off to religion and its accompanying troubles in a purely mate-

"Never Again!"

rialistic social system. Lately Russian Jewish emigrants have been preferring to come to the United States, rather than to Israel, for what they consider a better life. Their Jewish feelings are dead and Israel looks to them like a lot of work, which it is. In some cases Russia has accomplished the nearly impossible—turning off Jews to Judaism. Those Russian Jews who do come to Israel have a built-in aversion to the gospel in any form.

So Israel's diverse mixture of immigrants, who have in common their mistreatment by so-called Christians, is not very ready for the gospel. Any newly organized nation is largely made up of immigrants and its policies will reflect the feelings of those immigrants.

We are not supposed to resist a challenge as Christians, and certainly not *this* challenge. Where did our Lord Himself choose to witness, after all? To whom did He come? To whom did He first send the Holy Spirit?

The Lord knows the Jews are as resistant as ever, but He always embraced Israel. Paul went to the Jews first (even though his apostleship was to the Gentiles), tirelessly speaking to the Jews of foreign lands, getting kicked out of synagogues, doggedly explaining the Scriptures, and hopefully promoting a witness to the Gentiles through the saved Jews. The Book of Acts records his travels among the Jews and how they ultimately brought Christianity to the rest of the world. Peter was appointed as the special apostle to the Jews.

How have we forgotten so completely?

9.
"Why Do the Christians Hate Us?"

I felt a definite twinge of disappointment as I looked over the crowd that assembled on the first night of our Bible teaching at the YMCA. There were few Jews among them.

They looked like the same old group of gentile Christians I usually teach at any American church. "Why did you bring me all the way here?" I wanted to ask God. "I meet with these people week in and week out in Dallas."

There were the fine old Christian married couples, dressed as if for a banquet and carrying well-thumbed King James Bibles. There were the younger, enthusiastic believers, out to change the world for Christ overnight; they were in denims and worn-out sweaters. They typically carry the New American Standard Bible (NASB) translation of the New Testament. And there were the pale and stalwart old "deacons," as I always think of them, solemn and careful about their Christianity and always making sure that everything is seemly and fitting. They usually don't bring Bibles at all.

And there were, thankfully enough, those Christians in their middle years who deeply enjoy a well-developed relationship with the Lord. They carry the complete NASB with the pages fully marked with tiny notes, or a weather-beaten Scofield's with markers hanging out.

Someday I'm going to do a survey of Christians and their Bibles. I think you can peg the believer by the Bible he carries, or doesn't carry, and you could become expert enough to know his denomination and what he believes about eternal salvation, predestination, and election just by the translation he favors.

There were one or two cultists carrying pamphlets in addition to their Bibles. They hand out their literature at Bible studies in order to persuade people to worship on Saturdays, call God *Yahweh*, or some such favorite of their particular group.

I looked over the group face by face, looking for the olive skin and curly hair that would normally mark a Jew. (Israelis can fool you though; coming from every part of the world, they turn up as blonds, redheads, and even Orientals and blacks.) I found a half-dozen Jews among the seventy-five people that turned out for the opening night, and I assumed by the fact that they brought Bibles with them that they were already saved.

From where did we turn up such a multitude of Gentiles? Well, the "times of the Gentiles" are not yet finished in Jerusalem, of course, and they come out of the woodwork for Bible studies. We were obliged to do the opposite of Paul's technique—we had to reach out to the Jews by talking first to the Gentiles.

We determined to show those whom God brought

"Why Do the Christians Hate Us?"

how to develop the Scriptures for the Jews. We would show step by step how to demonstrate the gospel from the Old Testament and from prophecy. (Much of what is said in the New Testament and by the Lord Himself is now coming to pass in Israel.)

But would we ever get the Jews to come out?

Actually, we did have more Jewish people as the week went on, particularly for the film night. Though our ads ran in all of the Jewish publications in Jerusalem, we didn't really expect the Jews to respond to an offered Bible study. It is almost a sacrilege for Jews to sit down to a public Bible study—that's a completely Christian tradition. In Judaism, only the rabbis are competent to interpret the Scriptures and we weren't advertising any rabbinical teaching. (Many American Jews respond to a biblical witness by saying, "Well, that's what *you* say the Bible means, but as for me, I will have to ask my rabbi.")

American Christians feel that the Jews are very knowledgeable of the Old Testament. They think they'll have to prepare to answer to every detailed point about the law and the prophets in order to progress to the New Covenant and the Messiah. But actually, most Jews, rabbis included, haven't even a rudimentary understanding of the Old Testament. I have "debated" rabbis on the law and the prophets, but they weren't real debates since my opponents had only the vaguest knowledge of the Scriptures. Now if you want to talk about commentaries, that's another story. The rabbis usually have a thorough knowledge of what other rabbis before them have said about the Scriptures. But as to the Scriptures themselves, most

The Underground Church of Jerusalem

Jews either do not take them seriously at all, or depend on the local rabbi for the "proper interpretation."

Mal uncovered some of those "tell me what it says" Bible students in Jerusalem with his incisive study of the Abrahamic Covenant. One would suppose that people who live in the land guaranteed by that covenant would be familiar with the land grant, but many were surprised by Mal's revelations. We heard the familiar "cracking-of-the-binding" sound as old Bibles, which might have been passed down for generations, were opened to key Old Testament passages for the first time. There were audible gasps of appreciation as long-term Christians realized for the first time in their lives that their *whole* Bible was deeply relevant and their lives in Israel entirely predicted and guaranteed.

On the literature table we laid out Mal's book covering the material in the seminar and Hal Lindsey's *Late, Great Planet Earth* in Hebrew, hoping to cover both languages with dynamite learning. The cultists slipped their pamphlets onto the table or stood around handing out their material nearby after the lesson. And everybody milled about afterwards as if to pounce on an unsaved Jew should one dare show his face.

I had launched into my message the first night, apprising the local Christians that God has an organized way of going about His affairs with men; it seemed to be received with due appreciation. But it was Mal's thoroughgoing picture of the life of Abraham that really got to these pilgrims, who undoubtedly had traveled through Hebron and Mambre many

"Why Do the Christians Hate Us?"

times and had stood at Abraham's well and the other sites of that great patriarch.

We were off to a good start, though for all the Jews knew, we hadn't even hit town yet.

Interestingly, some of the folks we were teaching in our humble setting at the YMCA had gone during daytimes to the *sookas* throughout Jerusalem. Those are the "booths" of Leviticus 23:42 in which the Israelites are supposed to worship and dwell during the week-long Feast of Tabernacles. Some of our people took up their palm branches and went to fellowship in the booths. The booths symbolize God's sheltering of His people in the wilderness (Lev. 23:43) and the Israeli Jews, as well as those of America, love to build the little huts and worship in them.

There was a *sooka* put up at the apartment complex where I stayed and the folks in the building used it constantly, particularly the little children, who loved the trimmings. It was more like a clubhouse to them and they greatly rejoiced.

For the benefit of the people who might have no access to a private *sooka*, the city of Jerusalem had constructed one of magnificent proportions and beautiful decor by the Jaffa Gate. It was almost as big as a gymnasium and had gorgeous rugs and tapestries in addition to the prescribed branches and fruits which hung from the ceiling.

Only in Jerusalem can you go from a municipal *sooka* to a Christian Bible study in the same day. God still loves this city, to say the least. He has it marked out for the kingdom as the ruling city on earth, but we sometimes fail to appreciate the stunning concept that he will not part with it even in eternity. He will make "a new heaven" and "a new earth," indeed, in revamping His entire creation, but He will also provide "a new Jerusalem" to go with them! (Rev. 21:1–2). That's what you call being faithful to your city. That's real love.

Mal and I were very pleased with the turnout, whatever the particular leanings in the faith. We would have preferred, of course, to teach utter unbelievers—unsaved Jews—but to impart the valuable Old Testament information and prophecy to whomever we could was a privilege in Jerusalem. The cultists, the marginal believers in the crowd, and the few unsaved were certainly all a blessing to us.

And we perceived that we had a winner of an idea by the time the first evening ended. There were many good questions and the response was enthusiastic. Many people bought the books for further study and several asked me where they might obtain my other books dealing with Jewish evangelism.

We did not fear official intervention in what we were doing even though evangelism, which we were plainly advocating, is unacceptable to the government. We were tourists and the government has no recourse against tourists. It should be stressed that *anyone* can witness, teach, baptize people, and do any sort of Christian activity he wishes as a *visitor* in the land. You may not be the most popular person on the block, but you will not be sent home or otherwise legally interfered with. Of course, if you have a visa permitting you to stay over an extended period, then the government *does* have recourse over what you do and may cancel your visa. This has happened to some Christians.

"Why Do the Christians Hate Us?"

This situation is to be contrasted with what goes on with tourists in the Iron Curtain countries, China, the other Asian nations, and the jungles of the world. There visitors can run into real trouble for representing Christ—even trouble from the local churches or cults. The illustration of the missionary boiling in the pot is the clearest picture of local resistance to the gospel. The Communists tend to shepherd their tourists around on exact schedules with an eye to avoiding such nonsense as any evangelistic efforts.

What I mean to stress here is that Israel is fair to visitors, allowing them the freedom to do as they please within the bounds of the laws of the nation, and with much more ease than in many other places. Some Christians like to rationalize that the Israeli government persecutes Christians but the last case I can remember was Paul's trial. As a tourist, you are perfectly safe witnessing for Christ in Israel.

So go over there and tell a Jew about the Lord. God won't be offended.

Now Mal and I did have some fears about the reaction of the local audience, especially on film night when we had a full auditorium. We were only two against the multitude on that night, and the multitude might not have liked the goings-on. The government doesn't tell its people what to think or what they have to like over there, and it doesn't make a special effort to protect evangelists.

We counted on the YMCA personnel to exercise normal security measures if we ran into a problem. They were quite noncommittal about our whole program, never inquiring about what we were going to do in the room we rented and acting as if they never saw our ads (even though they posted them on their activities board). They socked Mal with a twenty-eight percent tax for paying his bill in Israeli money, which seemed a bit hostile to a good customer. (So eager are they to have the more steady American dollars that they punish outsiders for paying in local currency.) But they generally let us go our own way, treating us courteously and officially.

I had hoped to witness to Jewish YMCA personnel since I assumed they would ask about what we were teaching, but they couldn't have cared less if we were promoting Satan worship. To them, it was just "another day, another dollar," preferably an American dollar.

Breaking the Ice

On the second night a few more Jewish people came out. Perhaps the word had gotten around that we weren't conducting human sacrifice or an inquisition after all. They were recognizable not only by appearance but by the way they sat motionless and without Bibles, seeming to skeptically evaluate the performance rather than to listen to the message. I was very glad they came and I launched into my explanation of the seven feasts.

I had high hopes for the feast message convicting a Jew or two, but they showed little reaction one way or the other. I had at least looked for a good argument: "How can you apply what is clearly Jewish to something that is Christian? How can you say *Jesus* fulfilled *Jewish* feasts?" But it never came. Jews are like the wise old Indian chiefs we tend to portray in cowboy movies—silent, clever, and way ahead of you. I have

"Why Do the Christians Hate Us?"

no idea if any of my message hit home with any of the new listeners, but Mal's most certainly did. Mal stressed over and over again the debt owed to Israel by the world for Christianity—how the whole world should praise Abraham for his faith and his obedience to God; how the church of today should thank not only the apostles but the early Israelites who held the land and obeyed God and ratified the further covenants so that the Messiah came as planned. Mal admitted Jewish irreverence when it existed in the biblical record, of course, but he was emphatic on the Jewish contribution to world sanctification. That couldn't fail to impress an Israeli.

I finally got my chance to visit personally with an Israeli Jew on the third night.

He was the real McCoy (the real Goldberg or Cohen, I should say). He wore a skull cap and army fatigues and he listened to both of us most attentively. He seemed neither negative nor positive as I watched him through the evening, but he certainly took it all in. He was aware that people were watching him but that didn't bother him. He knew exactly what sort of Bible study it was before he came and he came to learn something.

He approached me right after Mal's conclusion and said, "If all the priests of the world would speak the way he does then Israel would listen."

I was delighted with this remark. He meant that if Christians would honor the chosen people the Jews might develop a real interest in Christianity, at least for the sake of a dialogue. But as things stand, his remark also implied, "Jews have no interest in those who snub them."

I determined to show that young man that Christians can be very kind to and respectful of Jews, but then I was not a normal representative of Christianity in his eyes. I was a Jew, and therefore not a "real" Christian at all. Real Christians are always Gentiles in the Israeli way of thinking.

I answered him, "There is no Christianity possible without Jews, according to the Bible. If all the 'priests' of the world understood Christianity as well as Mal does, then they *would* speak like him."

We spoke English and he had no objections to my opening my Bible. I invited him to accompany me down the hall to the lobby where we could concentrate on some Scripture. He was willing to listen, but was still very noncommittal.

I talked to him about Judaism and Christianity in general, using the Scriptures to back up my contention that what he thought of as two separate religions were virtually identical. We got into prophecy and he was very interested in whether Russia might invade Israel sometime in his future. He seemed to be watching me carefully and I hoped he would conclude, "Well the guy does believe what he says and it looks good on him."

The interview lasted about half an hour, during which time we covered quite a lot of Scripture. I brought out the New Covenant very clearly so that he could see that the worship of Israel today reaches back to a discontinued covenant (Jer. 31:32). But he was less interested in the technicalities of the Bible than in the human relations he had observed for the first time that night.

The man had simply never met Christians who were respectful toward the Jewish people.

"Why Do the Christians Hate Us?"

All he probably set out to do that night was to check whether our Bible study was hostile to Israel or not, and he went away from it with pretty good feelings.

And that's an accomplishment, considering the past relations of Christianity and Judaism.

Standing Room Only

On the fourth night we were overwhelmed with the film crowd, many of whom had come across the street from the King David Hotel. The 600 people included a large proportion of Jews this time; I suppose the drawing card was the Russian Invasion film.

With some people even standing along the back wall for lack of space, Mal got up and gave his introduction. I knew he had a lump in his throat, but I also knew he wouldn't say something like, "Praise Jesus that you all came tonight; we're here to save you." I was saying that in my heart, but Mal said something more accommodating to our curious onlookers.

He began by actually apologizing for the heavy evangelical emphasis in the films. We had been advised to do this—to at least qualify the material at the top of the program—by our pastor friend who had preached that Tabernacles message the previous Sabbath. He had told us, "Just make sure you don't appear to be sneaking in a witness. Tell them straightforwardly that you are an evangelical and that your material is Christian in emphasis. They won't mind it if you warn them, but don't try to fool them. Give them the chance to walk out on you at the beginning; then if they choose to stay, they know what they're going to get."

The Underground Church of Jerusalem

So Mal led off by saying something like, "These films are *about* Israel, *for* Israel, and *in favor of* Israel. I went to a lot of trouble and expense to make them. They're completely authentic, all made right here in your land. Every statement made throughout the two films is entirely biblical, taken from *your* Bible. Now there's a sort of Baptist church commercial along with each film, and that's just how it is. I'm a Christian, first and foremost, but I love Israel. And Zola and I will be up here afterwards for your questions."

It worked out fine. Nobody left. We all knew where we stood as the first film came on.

Mal gave me the credit for writing the Russian Invasion filmscript and I was secretly wondering if he planned to say in case of a riot, "Go get *him! He* did it!" But there was no riot and things progressed as if we were in any neighborhood movie theater.

I did see some young people leave shortly after the beginning of the Revelation film, which was screened first, but I assumed from their demeanor that they were thinking, "This place is dead. Let's go out and look for some action." Anyway, they didn't look offended, just bored.

Dead silence reigned as Hal Lindsey, narrator in the Revelation film, showed the vast destruction of planet earth and the vanquishing of Israel via Armageddon. The auditorium seemed tense and the people galvanized by the message. I had written some of Hal's speeches in the film and I had designed them to witness to the Jews. Now I thought I was going to be paid off for my efforts, one way or another.

I was gratified to see that no one left between films. Mal introduced the Russian Invasion film, again as-

"Why Do the Christians Hate Us?"

suring the crowd that the material was entirely biblical—Old Testament, in fact. I was again cited as the author, as if Mal were saying, "You have Zola Levitt to thank for this frightful invasion." But the film was shown without untoward incident, again before a rapt audience.

I looked forward to the part after the films when Mal and I would confront the questioners at the front of the auditorium. I assumed that only a handful of people would come forward, but instead we were completely surrounded. I was ready with my Bible, and I waded into a sea of difficult questions, as did Mal.

Two people stood out from the crowd as they asked their questions. One was an American Jewish lady, of the King David Hotel set for sure. The other was a Kabbalist.

The Jewish lady really jumped on me. "Why do the Christians hate us?" she wanted to know. Her question implied that she had understood all the good things we had said in the films about Christianity and its proper relationship to the chosen people. Indeed she was more than willing to accept the idea that she was due some respect from the true church. So she was a bit confused as to why the Jews have seemed to get nothing but derision and persecution from the "church."

It is a hard question to answer to the satisfaction of a Jew. No Christian following the Lord's commands could ever hate the Jews, of course, but how many Christians have really followed all of the Lord's commands? We pride ourselves on being baptized, on not drinking or smoking, on wearing conservative garments, on getting to church on Sundays, and on keeping a whole list of other outward displays of our faith, but when it comes to loving all men, I think most of us are guilty of disobedience. And when the Lord asks, "How did you treat my brothers?" much of the church will have to report, "Well we didn't accept them in our club and we certainly didn't vote them into office, and I didn't let my son or daughter date any of them, but gosh, my dentist was Jewish and I liked *him*."

The woman probably felt that Christians hated the Jews because she was told that as she grew up, possibly by European immigrants to America who came out of World War II. I know that was my case. My father didn't like Gentiles, and he failed to see any difference between "Gentile" and "Christians." I have talked about such matters previously, I realize, and I have thought about them ever since my coming to the Lord, but here I was faced with a direct question from a mystified and justifiably angry woman.

"I don't know," I told her. "But I'll say this: No one can hate the Jews and still love the Jewish Messiah."

She shrugged as if to say, "Just as I thought, they're all innocent," and left. That was sad. Here was a woman persuaded enough by the messages of prophecy and the respect for Israel shown in the films to come forward, but there was no way to answer her adequately about Christian aversion to the Jews.

When are we going to stop it?

Now the Kabbalist was a different story. Kabbala is a Jewish mysticism having to do with uncovering hidden secrets of God by means varying from analysis of the Scriptures to nearly occult practices. Kabbalists look into the Scriptures and the commentaries trying to find secret codes or messages-within-the-message. For instance, they might read the first letters of each line together and try to make new words and new thoughts. A Kabbalist once called me long distance and talked for over an hour; he thought he had discovered some sort of cryptic meanings in one of my simplest books. He said, "I now realize you're one of us." I asked him, "One of whom?" He sounded weird, like a cultist who worships psychic spirits.

The problem with Kabbala, as with so many other "hidden keys" to understanding God, is that it misses the simple point of the Scriptures. God has said what God has said; if you aren't finding God through His Word, then perhaps you aren't reading it with a teachable attitude.

That seemed to be the case with the intense young man who confronted me after the films. He deeply believed that Russia was going to invade Israel, but he had arrived at that by some extra-scriptural means. His question was about the allies of Russia, whom we listed in the film. "We must find out for sure who they are," he declared to me in a quavering voice that sounded as if we were going to hold a seance. "We must know—we must reach out for this fact and know it."

"Why don't you just read it in Ezekiel 38:5,6?" I asked him.

"What's that; what's that?" he asked. "It's in the Scriptures?"

"Sure it is," I told him, and whipped out my Bible. I read him the names of the allies as Ezekiel gives them, defining their present-day territories. He was dumbfounded.

The Underground Church of Jerusalem

"It's in the Scriptures," he muttered vaguely, as if to add, *"and all this time I've been consulting the stars."*

That young man probably communicated with the folks who fly the UFOs for all I know, but he had certainly never read Ezekiel. He thought you had to be mystical to know prophecy, but really, God isn't trying to keep any secrets from us.

We were truly relieved when the last of the crowd left the hall and we still stood there in one piece. Most of the questioners had dealt with us on a dignified level, respecting our "theories" and merely pressing for more information. They were as fair an audience of people who don't read the Bible as you would find anywhere else.

I think many of our original fears had come from watching what had happened at the soccer stadium immediately behind the YMCA earlier in the week. Israelis treat each soccer game in the same way football fans in the United States treat the NFL Super Bowl. It seemed that there was a big game that day and not enough seats, or maybe most of the crowd didn't have enough money to buy the seats that were available. In any case, a milling mob grew larger and larger by the ticket gate and two policemen eyed them warily. The end result was a rush on the place by the crowd—through the gate and even over the stadium walls. The policemen? They disappeared—off to issue parking tickets or something.

And we had figured that if the Israelis had no fear of their own tough policemen, how would they react to the visiting evangelists?

But, praise God, they were peaceful and they gave us a hearing. It was all we could ask for.

"Why Do the Christians Hate Us?"

The next night—the final night of our sessions—we were truly blessed. There were new Jewish faces in the crowd, brought presumably by the films. They still had some questions and, having seen our films, thought they might get something worth knowing from us.

It was the perfect night for those folks to come because Mal was into the prophecy part of his seminar, which deals with the Book of Revelation. I had finished explaining the seven feasts and was about to go into the exact details of the Russian invasion. God knows how to plan these things. We had scheduled our meetings in the auditorium for the only nights it was available—it worked out beautifully.

Mal sketched the horrors of the coming tribulation period as they are explained in Revelation and I tried to relate all possible current events regarding Israel and Russia to show how remarkably applicable the forecast of Ezekiel is to our times. I believe we made some people think that night.

The questions during the lesson were especially relevant, dealing as they did with hard, up-to-date issues. Nobody asked, "How do I go about getting washed in the blood?" but several of the Jews wanted to know where they could get more biblical information of this kind.

A Call to Action

Jews can get more biblical information from the people who know the Bible and that largely involves the true church. They can get more from you and more from your pastor and your church.

The Underground Church of Jerusalem

Two sources of what the Bible says for Israelis cannot be trusted at all—the rabbis and the liberal churches. There are rabbis and dead churches galore in the Holy Land, and their presence doesn't make one bit of difference as far as the biblical message is concerned. Neither group values or teaches what God has said. The Israelis can only know what the Bible says if they hear from those who read it.

Mal and I at least got their attention. But it was like trying to dye the ocean red by pouring in a glass of tomato juice at New York harbor. It's going to take a concerted effort on the part of the true church to get Bible knowledge, the gospel included, into the land it came out of originally. Israel at least deserves the same chance as any other nation.

We pour Bibles into Russia and we translate the Scriptures for a hundred other lands, but when was the last time you or some Christian organization sent a New Testament to Israel?

10.
"Message to America"

During 1976, America's bicentennial year, *Time* magazine ran a series of articles by heads of government around the world under the title, "Message to America." One of those articles was submitted by Israeli Premier Yitzhak Rabin (Dec. 20, 1976).

It may seem as though little Israel wouldn't have much to say other than congratulations to the mighty United States of America on its two-hundredth birthday. But Premier Rabin touched on an intriguing point: The two nations "graduated through the same school of ideas." Rabin pointed out:

> America's Declaration of Independence is separated from our own by 172 years. Though the class of 1776 and the class of 1948 came from different backgrounds and neighborhoods, they had learned the same lessons from the same old textbooks. They had common teachers who had taught them a system of ethics rooted in a single source, the Bible. They were so indoctrinated with the enlightenment of the Prophets—the abhorrence of injustice, the individual worth of every man and woman and the rights of the people to

The Underground Church of Jerusalem

liberty under the law—that it impelled them not merely to self-determination, but to actual revolution. For both, government by democracy was seen as the most natural system to protect the values that had inspired them.

The Premier went on to point out another similarity of the classes of 1776 and 1948—both nations were formed out of the tired and poor of the world. Both gave refuge to those persecuted for their religious beliefs; both were harbors of spiritual freedom.

> Both had an immigrant tradition. Persecution and the search for a better life had impelled them or their forebears to go on what Jefferson called a "quest of new habitations." Both conceived of their societies as havens for the homeless and the persecuted. For both, immigration became pioneering, and pioneering, nation building.

Let me digress to a letter sent to the Hebrew Congregation of Newport, Rhode Island, by an actual member of the class of 1776. The writer had visited at the Newport Congregation, the very first American synagogue, and he had been most cordially received. He writes:

> While I received with much satisfaction your address replete with expressions of esteem, I rejoice in the opportunity of assuring you that I shall always retain grateful remembrance of the cordial welcome I experienced on my visit to Newport from all classes of citizens.

"Message to America"

The writer continues in the vein of the American experiment in fairness to all citizens, which was a mighty young experiment at the time of this particular thank-you note. He cites with satisfaction that "the Government of the United States . . . gives to bigotry no sanction, to persecution no assistance . . ." and he concludes his letter scripturally, for the benefit of the Jewish congregation:

> May the children of the stock of Abraham who dwell in this land continue to merit and enjoy the good will of the other inhabitants—while every one shall sit in safety under his own vine and fig tree and there shall be none to make him afraid.

That letter is signed by the president of the United States, George Washington.

Now I call that good Christian-Jewish relations. President Washington obviously enjoyed his visit with America's first Jewish congregation, which was founded much earlier than most people would think. And he took pains to reassure the Jews of Newport that the government of their nation was very much aware of the problems of bigotry and persecution so keenly felt by those Jewish immigrants and Jews of all other times.

The Rhode Island Jews depended on good will from the American leaders, and the Jews of Israel still do.

What President Washington did not know was that the congregation at Newport was already anticipating trouble. Being experienced at the rigors of simply being Jewish, they had dug an underground tunnel leading from the altar of the synagogue to the harbor!

Boats were in readiness to take the first Jews away from this country should persecution get started here.

Fortunately, the Jews have remained relatively free of real persecution in this country and the escape route from the sanctuary at Newport was never used.

America was important to the Jews then as it is now. Bearing that in mind, let's return to Premier Rabin's article.

Rabin stated that America has a sober responsibility in today's world:

> So much of what America does (or fails to do), be it internal or external, must ultimately set off ripples, and sometimes waves, that interact with peoples far afield. . . . I see a nation [America] that still evokes moral principle in the diplomatic affairs of our world. To a small sister democracy like Israel, this is evidence enough to warrant the confidence that the United States will do good things for itself and for the world as its third century unfolds.

Of course the Premier of Israel wished to put the best foot forward in his article and Israel depends profoundly on the United States' friendship and support. But the article made a more important point, one that hits the heart. America and Israel *are* alike in many important ways. If a secular political leader can point out so many secular similarities between the two nations, how much more could people with Bible knowledge see deep spiritual similarities.

What was America at its beginning except a haven for true Christians? Was not our nation founded

"Message to America"

"under God" by prayerful men seeking to separate the church and the state so that the church might never have to go underground? Didn't it actually work out that way, with America becoming the Christian citadel of the world and sending missionaries abroad by the tens of thousands? Have we not developed the world's most impressive array of free and open houses of worship, protecting the good and the bad from oppression of any kind?

Then let us Americans not forget that the true Christian church of Jerusalem has to function "underground" even while secular Israel enjoys our fiscal and military protection. Remarkably, American Christians who feel the genuine kinship to a sister democracy and support Israel politically still fail to support her courageous biblical church.

We have been willing to send dollars and guns, but not the gospel.

God Loves Israel

Look at it this way—God cares. He took the trouble to reassure us over and over again that Israel was His Holy Land, Jerusalem His holy city, and the Jews His holy people. Apathy about Israel is like apathy about God, or about one of His most beloved relationships. It's unchristian.

Several times in history the Jewish people themselves had a choice of caring about Israel or not caring. When they were first about to enter the Promised Land after the exodus from Egypt, they hesitated because they were afraid to trust God. Those faithless people perished while wandering in the wilderness. Obviously they should have heeded God's own admonition about taking what He gave to them when He gave it. Then again, after the Babylonian captivity, Cyrus released the Jews to return to Israel as they liked, but only a remnant went. Those who returned to the land accomplished the rebuilding of the holy temple and the holy city, and they were there to receive the Messiah when He came. Those who stayed behind and bet their fortunes on Babylon lost out again, trusting in a pagan land that shortly became extinct. Finally, after the Roman conquests of the first and second centuries, the Jews had a choice of going or staying, though admittedly the Romans had made Israel a nearly impossible place for Jews. Almost every Jew fled in the great dispersion of Israel, as prophesied. But a tiny remnant did cling to the land through all those centuries; Jews could always be found somewhere in Israel, through the times of the Romans, the Moslems, and the Turks.

They were there to see the greatest Jewish miracle since Pentecost—the restoring of God's people to their land.

Choose the land, Christian! Stick with Israel.

But how? What should you do? It's hard enough to help distant peoples who *want* your help, I realize. And now I am asking you to help people who do not want the kind of help I am asking you to give. They don't want your Lord, your church, your witness, your New Testament, your missionaries, or anything else but your occasional cash when you drop by on a tour.

Never mind. God has told you what they need.

"Message to America"

Remember where He Himself chose to go when it came time for Him to walk among men?

I suggest you start by cultivating at least one close relationship with a Jewish person. Perhaps you already have a Jewish friend, but if not, be open to the opportunity when it arrives. Pray that God would give you the chance to befriend a Jew.

There is a reason for my asking you to do this. I want your Christian influence to rub off on a Jew. If it does, it will someday reach all the way to Israel. Every Jew in the world is connected to Israel through a heavenly heartline; God made it so. Your witness, your friendship, and your Christian humanity will make a difference. Jews need friends; they've always had a shortage.

Now if you are a Christian who does not like Jews, then my request goes double for you. Perhaps you have heard some monster stories about the Jewish people and so you have never given them a chance. But God loves these people whom He originally chose. Surely He can teach you to love them too.

As you relate to your Jewish friend, your religious preferences will come up and that is good. He is not going to run away if you mention church or the Lord. Jews are brought to Christ just as anyone else is—by experiencing Christian love, hearing the Christian gospel, and observing Christian fellowship. Love them to begin with. They will respond to that, believe me. Then tell them you believe the Bible—*their* Bible. Then, if possible somewhere down the line, take them to your church—without fanfare and without lots of phony handshaking. Simply show them that Christian people are normal, spiritual human beings.

The Underground Church of Jerusalem

Don't try to show them that Christians are *superior* human beings. It is neither scriptural nor true.

When you do all these things you will be doing what some missionaries call "pre-evangelism." Some unbelievers need to be prepared for evangelism itself and this is true of nearly all Jews today, due to their past treatment at the hands of Gentiles.

What I would expect to happen, if everyone reading this book carried out this simple request, is that numbers of Jews would eventually see that Christians are ordinary human beings with hearts and minds, hopes and dreams, even like Jews. A few Jews will be unimpressed or even unapproachable, but most will react amicably with fairness, discovering for the first time that Gentiles can be accepting and warm people. (Don't snort at this. I was brought up to think Gentiles were practically wild animals and my father had the evidence to back it up! Some lost ground has to be made up at this point.)

Now, out of that group of Jews that will have discovered that Christians make good friends, a few will look deeply into what makes a Christian. And some will be saved.

Those are the ones who will revolutionize the witness to Israel. Those are the ones who can bring the church of Jerusalem out of hiding and back into the sunlight of that Pentecost morning. Working from here or going over to Israel, saved Jews will make the difference.

Israel is a fair-minded nation and a democratic one. The majority rules in Israel but the minority has an important voice too. When a reasonable proportion of the people are believers, they will have a voice and a

"Message to America"

vote. Remember the orthodox Jews—they are far from being a majority in Israel but they deeply affect her policies and they are taken very seriously. Room will be made for any minority in that land—that's just the kind of place it is.

Sending the gospel to Israel, even through the local Jew, depends on you, Christian. Just remember, you are here today as a believer because of what *they* did during the first century.

I have another suggestion I hope a lot of people will heed.

Get involved with a mission to the Jews.

We do have a few in this nation, even if they don't get much attention. Chances are you go to a church where they would have Zola Levitt speak only once, but as an individual you can still support a Jewish mission. Even if Jewish evangelism is not popular in your group, remember that heavy cross the Christians carry in Israel. The mission to the Jews needs *you*, brother and sister!

Here is a listing of Jewish mission groups with which I have been personally involved. I can recommend them all. The addresses are below, and I don't mind if you put this book down right now and begin your letter writing. Whatever you may want in the way of tracts and biblical information about witnessing to the Jews, personal help, training or counsel on the matter, or perhaps Jewish Christian worship services in your area can be provided by the following groups:

The Underground Church of Jerusalem

The American Board of Missions to the Jews
460 Sylvan Ave.
Englewood Cliffs, N.J. 07632

Jews for Jesus
Box 3558
San Rafael, CA 94902

Messianic Jewish Movement International
7315 Wisconsin Ave.
Washington, D.C. 20014

The Friends of Israel
475 White Horse Pike
West Collingswood, N.J. 08107

All of these groups have a vast outreach in this country and abroad. The ABMJ is active in Jerusalem and Tel Aviv, and is the largest of the Jewish Missions. All of them are deeply tied to Israel.

Finally, there are Israeli consulates in the larger cities whose personnel are very eager to tell you whatever you would like to know about the Holy Land. There is much literature available which you can pick up in person or receive by mail; the personnel of the consulates are invariably gracious and friendly.

I recommended earlier that you go on a tour to Israel, which would, of course, give you the best possible idea of what goes on over there. That is still a fundamental part of witnessing to the Jews if you can afford it.

And pray. It would take only a moment for you to include the chosen people in your prayers each day. So many have cursed them for so long. Even some misguided Christians curse them. Little tracts come

"Message to America"

out all the time saying that the Jews of today aren't really Israel of the Bible, or that America is the new chosen people, or that there is a Jewish conspiracy to take over this or to undermine that. Offset these odious curses with prayer on behalf of the Lord's brothers. Thank the people who copied out the Scriptures and preserved them so faithfully for you, and whose original witness created the Christian church of the world. "Pray for the peace of Jerusalem . . . (Ps. 122:6)," the psalmist asks.

Let me give you another hymn I wrote on a sheet of paper on our plane ride home. After writing the one that appears at the beginning of this book I felt better. I sat back in my seat realizing that I would indeed be going home someday, returning to my brothers in Jerusalem. "God will bring me to Jerusalem," I had written in perfect conviction, and I was feeling happier with that thought.

I thought back to the Feast of Tabernacles, that timeless joy that could be seen on every street in the holy city during my visit. Praise God that He has chosen to have His people endure forever! The Jewish feasts are still going on in *Eretz Yisroel*, the land of Israel, I thought happily. Thousands of years ago, they went on every year without fail, and now it's happening again. As it was in the times of King David, it is again, and that made my heart glad. People there still wish each other, *"Hag Sameach!"* (Happy Holiday!)

I expressed this song then, and I give it to you.

The Underground Church of Jerusalem

Hag Sameach v'shalom!*
Happy holiday, my friend, and welcome home!
Blow the *shofar*, ring the bell
For the Jewish feasts are going on in *Erezt Yisroel*.

Hag Sameach v'shalom!
Happy holiday, my friend, and welcome home!
Tell the whole world, the whole world tell,
That the Jewish feasts are going on in *Eretz Yisroel*.

Hu Adon, Hu Adon!
Yeshua Hamashiach, Hu Adon!
Hag Sameach v'shalom
Yeshua Hamishiach, Hu Adon!

*Hag Sameach, Happy Holiday. *v'shalom*, and welcome. *Shofar*, ram's horn (trumpet). *Eretz Yisroel*, the land of Israel. *Hu Adon*, He is Lord. *Yeshua Hamashiach*, Jesus, the Messiah.

Hag Sameach

Words and Music by
Zola Levitt

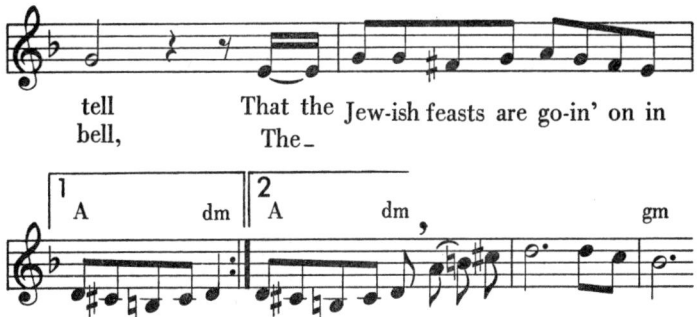